Charles Cuthbert Hall

Into His Marvellous Light

Studies in Life and Belief

Charles Cuthbert Hall

Into His Marvellous Light
Studies in Life and Belief

ISBN/EAN: 9783337253554

Printed in Europe, USA, Canada, Australia, Japan

Cover: Foto ©Lupo / pixelio.de

More available books at **www.hansebooks.com**

INTO HIS MARVELLOUS LIGHT

Studies in Life and Belief

BY

CHARLES CUTHBERT HALL, D. D.

MINISTER OF THE FIRST PRESBYTERIAN CHURCH
OF BROOKLYN, N. Y.

SECOND THOUSAND

BOSTON AND NEW YORK
HOUGHTON, MIFFLIN AND COMPANY
The Riverside Press, Cambridge
1893

The Riverside Press, Cambridge, Mass , U. S. A.
Electrotyped and Printed by H. O. Houghton & Company.

TO

THE MEMBERS OF MY CONGREGATION,

IN THE FIFTEENTH YEAR

OF OUR FELLOWSHIP IN

THE GOSPEL

OF JESUS CHRIST.

CONTENTS.

CHAPTER		PAGE
I.	INTO HIS MARVELLOUS LIGHT	1
II.	CHRIST THE PILLAR OF LIGHT	19
III.	THE LIMITATIONS OF LAW	35
IV.	THE JOYS THAT ARE PURCHASED BY SORROW	53
V.	THE ELEMENT OF SILENCE IN PERSONAL RELIGION	71
VI.	THE MINISTRY OF CHANGES	89
VII.	THE EMBRACE OF GOD	105
VIII.	THE PERSPECTIVE OF RIGHT LIVING	123
IX.	THE BENEDICTION OF THE RISEN LORD	141
X.	THE UNFORGOTTEN LABOURERS	159
XI.	THE GIFT OF ADVERSITY	177
XII.	THE SPLENDID IDEAL	195
XIII.	THE MOUNTAIN-CLIMB OF LIFE	213
XIV.	CHRIST'S KNOWLEDGE OF OUR SINCERITY	231
XV.	THE RETROSPECT OF TRIAL	247
XVI.	THE FAITHFUL COMPANION	265
XVII.	FORBEARANCE	283
XVIII.	THE RECOGNITION OF DEPARTED GREATNESS	301
XIX.	THE GLORY OF YOUNG MEN	317
XX.	THE INTERPRETER	337

I.

INTO HIS MARVELLOUS LIGHT.

I.

INTO HIS MARVELLOUS LIGHT.

"Into His marvellous light." — 1 PETER ii. 9.

HE who would attain great things must first believe great things. "To him that hath shall be given, and he shall have more abundantly." Great lives can be traced back to great aspirations. Ignoble and barren ideas of life do not produce rich and fruitful lives. Men do not gather grapes from thorns nor figs from thistles. Those who in any calling accomplish the higher possibilities of that calling are those who from the first have realized that those higher possibilities exist. The water of the stagnant pool has no energy to rise. The stream that comes bounding from the mountain has in itself power to bound heavenward again in the fountain. Mountains and fountains are essentially related. High springs are the birthplaces of vigorous powers. In all legitimate callings he who succeeds is he who has had high conceptions of success. In the Christian calling this is true. The great Christian lives have felt from the beginning that Christian life is great; that the light into which the Lord calls us is no "common light of day," but, indeed, "His marvellous light."

I would speak to you of some glorious possibilities of Christian experience. "Into His marvellous light." By each of the three chief apostles, John, Paul, and Peter, the splendid possibilities of Christian experience were fully realized. Each has described, by a characteristic title, Christian experience as it looked to him. John calls it "the everlasting life;"[1] Paul calls it "the glorious liberty;"[2] Peter calls it "the marvellous light."[3] We are not surprised to find these men becoming great Christians, when their views of Christian experience were so high and wide and great. They saw the greatness of their calling, —

> "And by the vision splendid
> (Were) on (their) way attended."

They tried to live out toward the measure of life's possibilities. In this they were not alone. Many have done the same, many are now doing the same, — believing great things and always living toward great things. To us the

---

[1] St. John iii. 16, 36; iv. 14; v. 24; vi. 27, 40, 47.
[2] Rom. viii. 21.
[3] 1 Pet. ii. 9.

Christian life has not grown dull, formal, conventional. It has grown newer and greater; in spite of all the many things in our common existence to hold one back, and keep one down, and beat out one's courage, and blunt one's spiritual perception, and "call the glory from the gray," the Christian calling is to-day God's marvellous light, more wonderful ever as the years pass, lighting up along the avenues of our experience glorious possibilities of knowledge, of direction, of endowment, of support.

Whoever is led to some particularly luminous and happy word wherewith to describe a great experience earns the thanks of all whose privilege it may afterwards be to share that experience. He thus becomes a voice through which many souls utter themselves. We thank the Apostle Peter for his description of the Christian calling. That word, "into His marvellous light," tells magnificently what they find that calling to be who realize its possibilities.

Truly God's marvellous light! How marvellous this light in contrast with darkness! — "Who hath called you out of darkness into His marvellous light." Contrast the situation, the moral atmosphere, the motives, the high and holy enjoyments, the goodly fellowships, the eternal consolations, the brilliant destiny of one who walks and lives in God's marvellous light, with the situation, the atmosphere, the motives, the pleasures, the fellowships, the destiny of one who walks in bestial, profligate, sensual darkness.

How marvellous this light in contrast with the cold twilight of commonplace, conventional experience! All the difference lies between them that lies between one of our most sullen, humid, relaxing, sunless winter days and one of our dry, clear, buoyant, glorified and glorifying mornings of the early summer. They who have lived in the twilight of conventional religion, acknowledging the routine, but discerning nothing in the substance of their faith to excite wonder or joy, cannot conceive the exhilarating happiness of the higher Christian experience when the liberty is *really* "glorious," and the sight is *really* "marvellous."

But we wish to examine in detail some of those glorious possibilities of experience which may unfold themselves to one and another who are called of God's Spirit into His marvellous light. We wish to point out how in a glad and clear Christian experience we may be made far richer and completer than we were before. And I know of no better way to illustrate our theme than to bring forward four types of experience which were realized respectively by four great lives at moments when they stood peculiarly unshadowed in His marvellous light. Their experience, unique for each one of them in respect of the circumstances which attended it, furnishes, in respect of the power realized in it, incalculable encouragement and hope to the Christian of to-day who is walking in the light, as Christ is in the light.

Peter, Paul, John, and Stephen, each in his own life, met an hour when he realized especially the blessing of the marvellous light, and when his experience therein created a magnificent suggestion and encouragement for us. Peter's supreme experience of the marvellous light was on the mountain of the Transfiguration;[1] Paul's was on the road to Damascus;[2] John's was on the island of Patmos;[3] Stephen's was in Jerusalem, at the hour of his intense trial and his victorious death.[4] Each, in his special hour of marvellous light, discovered a glorious possibility of Christian experience. When he stood unshadowed in the marvellous light, Peter realized the meaning of spiritual knowledge; Paul realized the meaning of spir-

[1] St. Matt. xvii. 1–9.
[2] Acts ix. 1–8.
[3] Rev. i. 10–20.
[4] Acts vi. 8–vii. 60.

itual direction; John realized the meaning of spiritual endowment; Stephen realized the meaning of spiritual support.

Peter, with the sons of Zebedee, stands before the Lord on the mountain top, called without warning into His marvellous light. An utterly new conception of the Person of Christ is imparted to him in that hour. He sees the fashion of his Master's countenance altered, His face shining as the sun, His raiment white and glistening; and, under the power of emotions he can neither resist nor control, he realizes the meaning and the influence of spiritual knowledge. Behold the new conflict of feelings within him. He is afraid, sorely afraid, bowed to the earth beneath the overshadowing cloud, beneath the sense of unfathomable mystery, beneath the lustre of Omnipotent glory. Yet he is also at peace. With the greater mystery has come a new-born calmness, a sense of having been admitted to something greater than the world can give, and although he measures not his words, nor hardly knows what they are, a new created consciousness of the blessedness of the new knowledge forces from him the confession, "It is good to be here."

His experience is indeed unique in respect of the circumstances attending it; but the substance of Peter's experience in that marvellous light of the Transfiguration is essentially the experience of all of us who, called from darkness into light, are finding out the meaning and the influence of spiritual knowledge. How unlike is the actual influence upon us of spiritual knowledge to that which we once imagined it to be! At the beginning of our Christian life we may have thought that the sense of mystery in connection with spiritual knowledge would pass away as we grew older, and that all things would become plain to us. At the beginning there were many things we could not understand; but, we thought, "I shall understand all presently." How different has been the real influence of advancing spiritual knowledge! If the Lord has called us, with advancing years, still farther into His marvellous light; if, as He gave to Peter a new and more magnificent view of the Person of Christ and of the relation of the law and the prophets to Christ, He has also given us brighter and fuller vision of the Lord; it is no more true of us than it was true of Peter, that the sense of mystery has passed away under the brighter vision of the truth. No! with the marvellous light has come to us, as to him, the marvellous cloud, the more overwhelming sense of the infiniteness, the unfathomableness of truth; of the wonderfulness of God; of the tremendousness of the Divine purpose; of the impossibility of comprehending all that God is, all that God means. Think not that spiritual knowledge means the clearing up of mystery; think not that spiritual knowledge means the reduction of the infinite truths of God to the easy and familiar terms of everyday life. Spiritual knowledge means to be drawn step by step into the marvellous light of the glory of Christ, and in that light to realize the overshadowing cloud of the infiniteness of truth, till a man sinks down before his God and worships with holy fear. But in that fear is peace. Though each step forward in the marvellous light unfolds more that overwhelms us, more that makes us feel how little we are, and how vast Christ is, we know that here, and only here, have we found the peace the world can neither give nor take away. Though pressed to the earth by the weight of truth we cannot grasp, of knowledge we cannot attain, the consciousness of having reached a nobler life burns within us, and our soul testifies to Christ, "Lord, it is good to be here."

"Into His marvellous light!" Saul of Tarsus is pressing on his way, impassioned with a mistaken purpose. Suddenly, without a warning, he is called out of darkness into Christ's marvellous light. As with a bolt from heaven, his old life, his old purpose, his old passion, are stricken to the earth. Out of the wreck rises a new man, blind to all behind him, blind to all around him, praying to Christ, "Show me what to do!" It is his crisis, his second birth. Standing unshadowed in the marvellous light, Paul realizes, for the first time in his life, the meaning of spiritual direction.

As of Peter, so of Paul, we may say that his experience is indeed unique, if we regard only the circumstances attending it; but we know that his experience in its substance has been that of others whose lives are brought to a crisis in the marvellous light. Paul is by no means the only person who has realized this possibility of Christian experience, even the full meaning of spiritual direction; who was going on in a certain course which he was satisfied to consider a right course; who was yielding himself up to a purpose which he was satisfied to call a proper purpose; who resented all criticisms upon his course and all interference with his purpose, till life was brought to a standstill by the call of God, speaking out of some providence or shining out of some truth.

Paul is not the only one who thought he had light, who persisted he had light, until the light came — God's marvellous light — to show him that he had been walking in darkness. Paul is not the only one who has been called into the marvellous light to realize there, suddenly and fully, the necessity of giving to life a total change of direction, and who has been conscious that that new direction could not be worked out from the past, a continuance of old lines; but must be a cutting and closing of old lines and a laying of new lines taken straight from Christ Himself. Who that has truly realized this experience of spiritual direction, — whether for him it has amounted to a total change of direction or has been but a bringing back to straightness of lines that had grown lax and crooked, — who, I say, has truly realized this experience of spiritual direction without looking back upon it in wonder and thankfulness? How extraordinary is the revealing power of that marvellous light when it has flooded our path in some moral crisis of life! How it divides the false from the true, exposing, with its unpitying glory, the miserableness of our fallacies, the weakness of our self-delusions; how it shows up the wrongness of wrong, till, though we have long trained ourselves to call evil good and darkness light, we can answer not a word! Yes, the sudden accuracy of the long distorted conscience in discerning between good and evil; the rapidity and exactness of self-conviction; the dissolving and disappearance of familiar shadows of conventional untruths, — these are the wondrous phenomena which attend the inrush of the marvellous light. How extraordinary and how precious is the directing power of that marvellous light when it has completed in us its unpitying work of self-revelation! Like some tremendous search-light at the mast-head of a man-of-war, when it has turned its awful beam upon the past, disclosing the mistaken way, the unholy delusion, the vanity, the sin, it leaves that past in darkness, abandoned and forgiven; it sweeps about and pours its glory into the future, streaming now upon a new path, a new way, a new direction, we had not seen, disclosing now new meanings, new motives, new delights we had not realized.

"Into His marvellous light!" The Lord's Day is spreading over Patmos its mantle of peace, where the lonely Apostle John waits the fulfilment of his exile. Perhaps, even to his obedient soul, the sense of the fruitlessness of his life is weighing upon him. Certainly, for his eagle spirit, it must have been a bitter thing to be caged on that silent rock, when his soul burned to speak a living word to a dying world. Believing, as I do, that the Revelation of John is earlier in time than the Gospel or the Epistles of John, you will see that as yet he had written nothing of that truth which none could write so well as he. On that still Sunday morning, as he walks and thinks, a Voice speaks behind him: "I am Alpha and Omega." He turns, and finds himself standing in the marvellous light. And out of the light comes the charge, the sevenfold charge: "Write, write, write the things which thou hast seen, and the things which are, and the things which shall be hereafter." Where is now the loneliness of the exile? Where is now the sense of the fruitlessness of life? Gone, forever gone. For the apostle has received his message. In the marvellous light John has learned the meaning of spiritual endowment. Henceforth life can have for him no indefiniteness, no scattering indirection. He has had his orders from his King. His life-work is laid upon him.

Is he alone in this? Is he realizing a possibility of spiritual experience which none of us may realize? Yes, alone, if you look but on the circumstances amidst which he received his message; alone, if you think but of the audible and visible phenomena of that glorious hour, — the voice that mingled with the sound of thundering waves, the glittering girdle, the illustrious countenance " as the sun that shineth in its strength."[1] But not alone, if you think of the substance of his experience rather than of its form. He is but one of many whom God has called into His marvellous light, that He might give them a message, to write or to speak or to live, for His sake and for man's sake. He is but one of many who know what it is to have heard a Divine call summoning them to the consecration of life, for the utterance of the truth and love of Christ; to utter that truth by a faithful, constant, self-denying service; to utter it by a pure and gentle ministry of influence, in their own homes, in their own social sphere, in the manifold labors of the church of Christ. Happy are they who can in any sense be conscious of having been called into the marvellous light of Christ, and of having there received a spiritual endowment, — a call, a charge, a message from Him Who has had prophets and apostles as His willing messengers. Can you feel that Christ has given

[1] Rev. i. 13, 15, 16.

you anything to do? Can you feel that He has laid any charge upon your life? given you aught to tell or show, in speech or silence to your fellowmen; aught to make plainer to the eyes that do not see His marvellous light? Be thankful, for in this you are treading near to the very holiest ground man has ever been permitted to tread!

"Into His marvellous light!" As one who stands tied to a stake, in the rising tide which must soon cover him, Stephen, the first of the deacons, stands in the rising tide of hatred and malignity which must soon sweep away his life. It is an awful hour, of fierce and unrelenting strain; immediate expectation of bodily pain, and of the mystery of death. With irrepressible curiosity the eyes of all the council are fastened on him to see if he will break or stand under the strain. "And looking steadfastly on him they saw his face as it had been the face of an angel." Why does he not break under the supreme strain of his life? What is that light upon his face? It is His marvellous light, the same that Peter had seen, and the same that John and Paul were yet to see. "They looked steadfastly on him." "But he, being full of the Holy Ghost, looked up steadfastly into heaven, and saw the glory of God, and Jesus standing on the right hand of God." In that marvellous light he realized, in the hour when he would most have desired to realize it, the full meaning of spiritual support. When the stones were raining upon him, he was praying "Lord Jesus, receive my spirit." When the cries of madness were raised about him, he was interceding, "Lord, lay not this sin to their charge." When the climax of confusion was bursting over him, "he fell asleep." What was his secret? What could raise him so far above his circumstances? What could keep him in perfect peace through all that bitter storm? It was that possibility of Christian experience which is within the reach of all who are standing in His marvellous light. Spiritual support: the grace that still keeps us from breaking, when the strain has reached the breaking-point; the power that still renews trust and love and hope when untoward circumstances have hedged us in and bound us fast; the love that shall still hold us fast with Everlasting Arms, till we fall into the blessed sleep, entering eternally into His marvellous light! Amen.

II.

CHRIST THE PILLAR OF LIGHT.

II.

CHRIST THE PILLAR OF LIGHT.

PREACHED ON EASTER DAY, 1891.

"I am the light of the world: he that followeth Me shall not walk in darkness, but shall have the light of life." — JOHN viii. 12.

A LIGHT. A moving light. A man following a moving light. And so my theme, this Easter morning, is and must be "Christ the Pillar of Light." For this is what He means when He says: "I am the light of the world: he that followeth Me shall not walk in darkness, but shall have the light of life." It was the Feast of Tabernacles, commemorating the journey through the wilderness. In the court of the women were blazing the great candelabra lighted in memory of the pillar of fire. Christ mounts the memory, and speaks from it as from a throne. "I am the light of the world: he that followeth Me shall not walk in darkness, but shall have the light of life." He loved to mount the greater memories of Israel, and to speak from them as from thrones, His own kingship over the lives of men. Is it the hoary memory of Abraham, the father of the faithful? Like a king He says: "Before Abraham was, I am."[1] Is it the memory of the manna in the desert? Like a king He says: "Your fathers did eat manna in the wilderness, and are dead. This is the bread which cometh down from heaven, that a man may eat thereof, and not die."[2] Is it the memory of the water pouring from the smitten rock? Like a king He says: "If any man thirst, let him come unto Me, and drink."[3] This morning He speaks to us from the pillar of light. He mounts that memory, and utters Himself from it, as from a throne. "I am the light of the world: he that followeth Me shall not walk in darkness, but shall have the light of life."

When, looking back to the desert of the exodus, we consider this memory, Israel's pillar of light, we find, on reflection, four reasons why, in the glorious field of resurrection truth, it becomes a worthy symbol of the risen Lord.[4] First, there was light. Second, there was moving light. Third, there was the lighting of the way. Fourth, there was the lighting of the follower.

[1] St. Jno. viii. 58.
[2] St. Jno. vi. 49, 50.
[3] St. Jno. vii. 37.
[4] Ex. xiii. 20–22.

First, there was light. Light in the pillar itself. It was not the glory of the sunset falling on it, and painting it with transitory color; it was not the glory of the moon, pouring over its surface a sheen as of burnished silver. The light was the immanent substance of the pillar; the glory was an underived glory, proceeding from itself. Whilst the common light of day remained, the pillar was a pillar of cloud, the stately witness of its own continuance; but when darkness overspread the wilderness, when landmarks vanished, and peril ambushed itself in shadow on every hand, then the heart of that cloudy shrine disclosed its interior and immanent glory, pouring light out upon the darkness.

Second, there was moving light. Onward moved the pillar, telling them the wilderness was not their home. Onward, ever onward, from encampment to encampment, from stage to stage; from palm-shadowed Elims of repose; from sultry deserts of scarcity; from hard-fought fields of battle,— still the light moved on.

Third, there was the lighting of the way. It was a perpetual revelation. Hour by hour new features of the wilderness disclosed themelves to the march of light. Paths before unknown were revealed beneath that searching glory. Precipices unsuspected were thrown out of shadow. Ambushes were unmasked, and safety travelled in the train of light.

Fourth, there was the lighting of the follower. The glory fell on every follower. They went through the desert not like prowling robbers, hating detection ; beams from the pillar of light flashed on the vestments of priests, on the spears of soldiers, on the trumpets of choirs, on the eager faces of men and women. Walking in the light, they became an army of light. He only lost the light who ceased from following.

Ask not, then, what Jesus meant when, standing in the Temple court in the Feast of Tabernacles commemorating that desert pilgrimage, He called Himself the light of the world. Ask not, then, what Jesus means when, meeting us who believe His resurrection and His risen life, He says to us, this Easter morning, to each man, each woman, each youth, who will receive His word : "I am the light of the world : he that followeth Me shall not walk in darkness, but shall have the light of life."

"I am the light of the world," — Christ the pillar of light. "He that followeth Me," — Christ the moving pillar of light. "He that followeth me shall not walk in darkness," — Christ the moving pillar of light, lighting up the way. "He that followeth Me shall have the light of life," — Christ the moving pillar of light, lighting the follower.

I. "I am the light of the world," — Christ the pillar of light. Christ is light, for Christ is God. God is light, and in Him is no darkness at all. Christ is God manifested. He is the effulgence of His glory. "He that hath seen Me hath seen the Father."[1] Christ is the light of the world. Coming into the world He has brought in Himself a light for every man. The Holy Spirit is the medium, through Whom, as through an atmosphere, the light is carried into the life of each soul. Whoever has the Holy Spirit dwelling in him sees the light by means of the Spirit. The Holy Spirit is not the light of the world; even as the atmosphere which transmits the sunlight is not the sunlight, but is the medium through which we receive the sunlight. Christ says: 'I am the light of the world." Christ is not the reflection of a light, as sometimes the windows of a house blaze with the reflection of the sunset. He is the light. The pillar of light in the desert was not bright with the

[1] St. Jno. xiv. 9.

reflection of sunset, nor with the reflection of moonbeams. Its interior and immanent substance was light. It was the underived source of light. It gave light where there was no light. So is Christ the pillar of light. Light is the immanent and underived substance of His being. It is impossible to walk in the unshaded presence of the sun's rays and not be in the light. It is impossible to walk in the unshaded presence of Christ and not be in the light; for He is the light; therefore He says, with the positiveness of one who formulates an axiom: "He that followeth Me shall not walk in darkness." This truth is the postulate of this Easter message. It is the truth assumed as the formation of further reasoning. Whoever grants this postulate, and so receives Christ as the underived and immanent light, is carried already to the conclusions which I have suggested. Whoever cannot grant this postulate, whoever is unable thus to receive Christ, not as a glorious reflection of some light exterior to Himself, but as in Himself and as of Himself light, is unable to accept the truths which rise from this foundation and pile themselves up before our eyes as a pillar of light. I plead with every soul which, on this Easter morning, pants for a more abundant, richer life, to grant this postulate which Christ Himself pronounces, when He says: "I am the light of the world."

II. "I am the light of the world: he that followeth Me," — Christ, the moving pillar of light. The pillar of light is not anchored in the desert, to stand forever in one place, a wonder of the world, a spectacle to be marvelled at by gaping crowds, or to be ignored by the absorbed and the indifferent. It has appeared for a purpose: to lead men on, shining upon their way, and shining upon themselves. Therefore it moves; it leads; it adapts itself to their necessity, which is the necessity of progress. It goes before them that they may follow. It precedes them into all new conditions and new scenes, that it may disclose those conditions and illuminate those scenes. So is Christ the moving pillar of light. Whoever keeps with Him must keep moving. To walk in His light is to be a follower. Forward is His watchword, and is ours. To go to men and lead them on is still His work. To all among us, in whom is His Holy Spirit, revealing the light, Christ is the moving pillar of light, the light that ever goes on — and on; that says to us by its own gloriousness, "Follow Me." Christ is energy as well as light, — a light that moves as well as a light that shines. "The dayspring from on high hath visited us, to give light to them that sit in darkness and in the shadow of death, and to guide our feet into the way of peace."[1] Behold with what energy the pillar of light moves when the stone is rolled away from the sepulchre, and the light becomes the light of the risen Lord. Behold how in the brief forty days between the Resurrection and the Ascension He is placing Himself before men to lead them onward, to lead them upward. The angel in the sepulchre testifies to the women of the moving pillar of light, saying, "He goeth before you into Galilee: there shall ye see Him."[2] On the Emmaus road we see the moving pillar of light placing Himself in touch with those two sad lives, and shining upon their way till their own hearts burn with answering light.[3] On the Ascension morning we see the moving pillar of light, leading them out as far as Bethany,[4] and then leading them up in heart and mind to that life more magnificent, —

"Where the glory brightly dwelleth,
And the new song sweetly swelleth,
And the discord never comes."

And to-day, so far as we realize the concep-

[1] St. Lk. i. 78, 79.
[2] St. Mk. xvi. 7.
[3] St. Lk. xxiv. 32.
[4] St. Lk. xxiv. 50.

tion of a risen Lord, Christ becomes to the individual the moving pillar of light; not a glorious memory, anchored in the desert of the past, not a distant splendor withdrawn by His Ascension to some inconceivable geographical remoteness; but a pillar of light, discerned not now with our fleshly eyes, as Peter and John discerned Him, but discerned by the revealings of the Holy Spirit, — a pillar of light Who is with us all the days, and Who still will lead us on,

> "O'er moor and fen, o'er crag and torrent, till
> The night is gone."

This is the presence of Christ, the moving pillar of light, Who has come to each of us, as He came to those two lives on the Emmaus road, to put Himself in touch with our experiences, and continually to lighten our darkness. If changes come to us, He has always anticipated those changes, and moved into relation with the new conditions. If our path suddenly and sharply turns to adversity, the pillar of light has moved into the valley before us; and if, in seasons of awful pining and repining, we seem driven through a dark, tempestuous sea, even there the moving light goes onward, and if we follow it, we reach the shore of peace again.

III. "I am the light of the world: he that followeth Me shall not walk in darkness," — Christ, the moving pillar of light, lighting up the way. "Thou wilt shew me the path of life."[1] It is nightfall in the wilderness, and every moment new veils of darkness are wound about the landscape. No natural light of sun or moon remains. Yet Israel must go forward; the forced march in the desert cannot be postponed; this is not their rest. Then through the gathering night appears that opalescent pillar, pouring forth the floods of its interior and immanent glory. And lo! the way appears; the darkness is smitten like the sea, and through the midst of gloom the moving pillar cuts a track of glory. Precipice, torrent, ambuscade, the fatal snares of darkness are disarmed, and by a way that they knew not Israel is led through the night. "I am the light of the world: he that followeth Me shall not walk in darkness." The moving pillar lights up the way for him who follows it. Life is a forced march through the desert, and has its hours of mingled necessity and fear, when natural light fails us at every step, when the gathering veils of uncertainty obscure the path more and more till it becomes impenetrable, yet when we know

[1] Ps. xvi. 11.

we must go on. We cannot encamp at twilight and wait till dawn. This is not our rest. Go on we must. Yet how to go, when all is dark before one; when no sunny ray of certainty falls upon the path; when no pale moonbeam of probability struggles through the shade; when the experience is unique and the path is untrodden! It is then the pillar of light begins to shine, and slowly to move onward; it is then the opalescent glory begins to pour into the night, lighting the way up, inch by inch, foot by foot, yard by yard. "He that followeth Me shall not walk in darkness." Onward moves the pillar, but only he who follows is saved from the darkness. There is a way out of every wilderness, — and there is a pillar of light to show the way out. But the condition of guidance is to keep in the presence of Christ. And to keep in the light is to keep moving, for the light moves. "He that followeth me shall not walk in darkness." To cease from following is to be left in the dark. "For with Thee is the fountain of life: in Thy light shall we see light." [1] Jesus lives! Jesus leads! Jesus lights! To follow is to see! The pillar moves. Passions, habits, perversities of judgment, the spirit of delay, fear, fond clinging sins, — these

[1] Ps. xxxvi. 9.

hold us back. Meanwhile the pillar moves. There is light, but light is going. Who will go, too? Who will cry this Easter morning, "Lord, we have left all and have followed thee?"[1] "If any man serve Me, let him follow Me; and where I am, there shall also My servant be."[2]

IV. "I am the light of the world: he that followeth Me shall have the light of life," — Christ, the moving pillar of light, lighting up the follower. It is midnight in the desert; rock ridges and sands are wrapped in common gloom; wild beasts, leaving their caves, prowl through the waste; robbers crouch secure, and watch more fiercely than beasts for their prey. Darkness everywhere and on all faces, save where the people of God are following the pillar of light. The light lights up the followers; on the vestments of priests, on the spears of soldiers, on the trumpets of choirs, on the faces of men and women, the light is falling, creating an army of light. So also Christ, the moving pillar of light, promises to them that follow Him another and a greater thing than guidance, — not only "they shall not walk in darkness," but this also, "they shall have the light of life." It is much to be guided by

[1] St. Mk. x. 28.   [2] St. Jno. xii. 26.

light; it is greater to be glorified by light. It is much to see the way by the light that shines from Him; it is greater when the light kindles our own eyes till they, too, shine with the light that is in His. He who follows the light of the world becomes a light of the world. He who said, "I am the light of the world," said also, "Ye are the light of the world."[1] For the pillar of light, which lights up the way for the follower, lights up also the follower in the way. What is likeness to Christ? Likeness to Christ is when the light from the moving pillar falls on the life following close behind it, till the following life becomes also in its way a moving pillar of light. "But we all, with unveiled face reflecting as a mirror the glory of the Lord, are transformed into the same image from glory to glory."[2]

"He shall have the light of life." Light is an attribute of our normal life, for God is light. Sin, sorrow, over-pressure, selfishness,— these are the great enemies of light, and so the enemies of a perfect life. Christ sorrows over our lost attributes. He has come to give them back. "I am come that they might have life, and that they might have it more abundantly."[3] To give us back those lost attributes

---

[1] St. Matt. v. 14.   [2] 2 Cor. iii. 18, R. V.
[3] St. Jno. x. 10.

of life, He loses His own life on the cross, and takes it up afresh on Easter morning. The conditions for the restoration of our lost attributes are now all supplied, save one, and that is left with us to supply: "He that followeth Me shall have the light of life." To keep in the presence of the risen Lord; to follow the moving pillar; to lay aside every weight and the sin which doth so easily beset us, to run with patience the race set before us, "looking off unto Jesus, the author and finisher of our faith,"[1] that is the restoration of the attribute of light. The glory of pureness, the glory of patience, the glory of grand endeavor, the glory of fellowship with God, are the light that is in Him; if we follow, it will fall on us, and as He is, so shall we be in this world. Amen.

[1] Heb. xii. 2 ; Gr. ἀφορῶντες.

III.

THE LIMITATIONS OF LAW.

III.

THE LIMITATIONS OF LAW.

"What the law could not do." — ROMANS viii. 3.

HUMAN law is the most majestic structure man has reared, the most tremendous instrument man has wielded. "The law," said Plutarch, "is queen of the gods and men." "Laws," said Montesquieu, "in their most general signification, are the necessary relations resulting from the nature of things."[1] The impressiveness of human law becomes particularly obvious when we station ourselves at certain standpoints from which to regard this great fabric. For example: Consider human law in respect of its foundation in the moral self-consciousness of man. The essential principles of law are not made by man. They are discovered by man as existing within himself. In his own moral self-consciousness he finds the foundations of law in the primary intuition of right. He has not laid those foundations: they are laid

[1] *Spirit of Laws*, Bk. I. Cap. I.

within him by his Creator. While man is man, law is law in essence.

Consider human law in respect of its accord with ethical perfection. The theory of law is the theory of absolute righteousness. The ideal of law is an ideal right: that man shall deal justly with his fellow-man; that none shall go beyond and defraud his brother in any matter; that every individual shall enjoy the recognition, or the protection, or the vindication of his rights; that society shall be framed in the beauty of a faultless order and clasped in the bond of peace.

Consider human law in respect of its passionless review of evidence. Law is passionless. It neither loves, pities, nor hates. It recognizes precedent, but not prejudice. In theory, it is no man's friend and no man's enemy. It sifts out opinions from evidence, that it may hold and weigh evidence alone. It is cold, hard, and white as the marble of Pentelicus.

Consider human law in respect of its penal momentum. Was it ever your fortune to stand on the deck of some smaller craft and watch the Umbria or the Lahn come up the Narrows from the sea; to note that awful silence of its momentum as it devours space? Did the momentum of that giant hull ever suggest itself to you as the product of a force within itself, yet not of itself, — a force of which the hull is the essential vehicle and expression? Such is the penal momentum of human law. A force within itself, yet not of itself. The limitless imperative of moral obligation confers on law a momentum which compels it to execute its own penalties. It has no choice but to protect the innocent, no choice but to punish the guilty.

Such, then, is the impressiveness of human law. Considered in respect of its foundation in the moral self-consciousness of man; or of its accord with ethical perfection; or of its passionless review of evidence; or of its penal momentum, it indeed may be called the most majestic structure man has reared, the most tremendous instrument man has wielded. Filled with these thoughts, it strikes us at first with surprise to behold that there are things which the law cannot do. Yet on reflection we see that there is a point beyond which this great instrument of human law is powerless.

Human law cannot forgive sin. A person may forgive another, but law cannot forgive. Horace Bushnell truly says of this, "The law, being impersonal, cannot of course forgive anything itself; or in any way compound its own wrong."[1] There is a pardoning power, but it is lodged with the executive government rather than with the judiciary. The judge who should attempt to arrest the penal momentum of law would be unseated from the bench.

Human law cannot abolish crime. That the law by its terrors diminishes the sum of crime is not to be doubted. But that it has no power to abolish crime is demonstrated by the daily history of society, and by the constant supply of inmates for our penal institutions.

Human law cannot regenerate the conscience or renew the affections. It may by its severity appeal to the sense of fear. It may by its dignity appeal to the sense of right. But its appeal is ever that of an external instrument, not that of an inward, regenerating power. We have no means of estimating the vast extent to which law restrains evil conduct; but we have no evidence that law has ever yet regenerated a motive, rehabilitated a corrupt conscience, or recreated in holiness an impure affection. These things, the forgiveness of sin, the abolition of crime, the regeneration of conscience, are among the things which (not-

[1] *Forgiveness and Law,* p. 93.

withstanding the impressiveness of human law) "the law could not do."

But when we lift our eyes thoughtfully and reverently from human law to Divine law, to the moral law of God, we find that neither can the Divine law do these things, although in its majesty it transcends all human law. "What the law could not do" is spoken, in our text, of the supreme conception of all law, even of the perfect moral law of God for the guidance of man. No human language can describe the majesty of God's moral law. All that we discern of solemn splendor in human law is but a reflection of the same attributes perfectly and primarily existent in Divine law. Divine law is founded in the Divine self-consciousness. What God has said to us in the commandments "Thou shalt" and "Thou shalt not" is not a list of technical regulations adopted by Him to show His power over us. These are the expression of moral necessities founded in His own being and revealed to His own self-consciousness. Rightness and wrongness are not rightness and wrongness merely because God says they are; they are (as Montesquieu says of human law) "necessary relations arising out of the nature of things." They inhere in the essence of God; and until God is destroyed, they cannot be destroyed. Says Faber in his noble hymn, "Right is right, since God is God."

Divine law represents moral perfection. Suppose God's will were done on earth as it is done in heaven. What an earth this would be! Moral perfection would rest like a diadem on every brow. Mercy and truth would meet together in every transaction of man with man. Righteousness and peace would kiss each other in every outgoing of man's consciousness toward God. The Divine law would be the rule of a sinless universe wherein every creature would fulfil a perfect destiny of usefulness, felicity, and holiness.

The Divine law is a passionless review of evidence. Shall not the Judge of all the earth do right? Shall not those clear, all-seeing Eyes read us as we are? Shall not that perfect Mind deal with us in equity? No passion, no resentment, no prejudice shall warp the law of Him who is all truth and all knowledge.

> "All shadows from the truth will fall
> And falsehood die, in sight of Thee.
> Oh, quickly come, for doubt and fear
> Like clouds dissolve when Thou art near." [1]

The Divine law carries in itself penal mo-

---
[1] The Rev. Lawrence Tuttiett.

mentum. Until God denies Himself, until God destroys that eternal imperative of moral obligation which is the substance of His own being, He cannot arrest the penal momentum of the moral law. It is the vehicle and expression of His own life. Were that force of law to be arrested, were that Divine imperative of moral obligation to be suspended, the moral universe drops with a crash; there is nothing left that is absolutely and objectively right; there is no right, there is no wrong, higher than public opinion; God has abdicated in favor of the moral anarchists.

And yet, we are told to-day, even of this Divine law, which is founded in the Divine self-consciousness, which represents moral perfection, which is a passionless review of evidence, which carries in itself penal momentum, — of this we are told that it has its limitation, that there is that which the "law could not do."

The Divine law cannot forgive sin. Having in itself that eternal imperative of moral obligation which proceeds forth from the eternal right in God's life, law can simply recognize facts and act upon them. It cannot reverse facts. On the one hand it recognizes obedience; on the other hand it recognizes disobedience. It cannot punish obedience without ceasing to be law; it cannot protect or remit or forgive disobedience without ceasing to be law.

The Divine law cannot abolish sin. For thousands of years man has known the law, yet look at man to-day. Over every metropolis of the world is the Divine edict, "Thou shalt not." Yet look at New York, and London, and Paris to-day. Over your life and mine, since we were children, have sounded like tremendous organ tones the commandments of God. Yet look at our conduct and at our secret thoughts, and confess what they have been.

The Divine law cannot regenerate the conscience and the affections. It is as pure and holy for the unconverted man as for the converted man, yet it does not make the unconverted man sorrow for his sin, or aspire for fellowship with God. It speaks to him in the language of moral perfection; he hears it with his outward ears, but in secret he is unchanged, satisfied with his sins, lusting after further enjoyment of them.

In view of these obvious limitations of law, of whose existence we are convinced by looking at our own hearts and at the world around us, it is necessary for a thoughtful being to do one of two things: to become a pessimist or to become a Christian.

A pessimist is one who holds that this world is the worst possible of worlds; that the destiny of man is the saddest of all possible destinies; that the terribleness of life is too great to be resisted. And indeed, if there be no redeeming offset to the limitations of law, the pessimist is right, and his sorrow is creditable to himself. For is not life too terrible to be described, is not its misery too vast to be uttered, if we and all men are living out our brief day, and rushing on to eternal night under a law which of necessity condemns us, yet has no power to forgive us, or to abolish our sin, or to regenerate us? If one is not a Christian, it is better, it is more honorable, it is less base to be a pessimist, than to be one of those who, in such a world, take their ease in a life of sin. Surely they are most like the beasts that perish who can live in pleasure without a faith which suggests some offset to the limitations of a law that condemns humanity, but cannot redeem it. I can conceive nothing more terrible than the situation suggested by those simple words of St. Paul: "What the law could not do." It can do so much to condemn humanity. It can do nothing to relieve humanity. It is like a surgeon who lays open the very vitals of his patient, and then withdraws, saying, "I leave you where you are; I can do nothing to relieve your agony." No wonder those who believe this are pessimists. Their pessimism is honorable to them.

But I refuse to be a pessimist. There is that in me, not myself, which whispers to me of a nobler destiny for myself and for my fellow-beings. The same power that has long convinced me of the fact of a Divine law, of the fact that God expresses Himself to me through those dicta of righteousness which are a part of His own substance, — that power is constantly telling me that God has come in (at the point where law fails through limitation) to offset the limitation of law by a new work, even the work of grace. Therefore I am not a pessimist, and because I am not a pessimist, I am a Christian. And my Christianity expresses itself in the answers to these two questions: What causes the Divine law to be limited? What are God's offsets to that limitation?

What causes the Divine law to be limited? Why are there things that "the law could not do"? The great answer to this question is found by reading on through the few words that follow our text: "What the law could not do, in that it was weak through the flesh." The flesh is the cause of the limitation, and in that sense the weakening, of God's law,—the sinful nature of man. If man were holy, as God is, and as God made man to be, he would need nothing more than the Divine law to keep him in righteousness, and so in blessedness forever. Every commandment of that law, proceeding out of the holy depths of the nature of God, would be perfectly appreciated and completely received in the heart of man, and as the clear, still water of the lake fully reflects the cloud-forms in the sky, the calm and clear moral nature of man would completely answer to the will of God. God would speak, and man's answer would be the echo of God's voice. God would command, and man's joy would be to do His commandments. And thus the sinless soul would find every need of its nature met and satisfied in the Divine law. It would need nothing but law for its guidance and for its bliss. But we are not like the calm, clear lake reflecting the sky; we are like the troubled, turbid sea when it cannot rest. The flesh, the flesh is our natural life: the things of the flesh, the laws of the flesh, the lusts of the flesh. This is *sin* in the nature of man, corrupting the conscience; demeaning the affections; nourishing selfishness; catering to pride; seducing the will. This is "the flesh," and we that are in the flesh cannot please God; we are not anxious to please God; we do wish to please ourselves. What can the Divine law, great as it is, do for us? It cannot forgive us; it cannot regenerate us; it does not appeal to us; it can only condemn us. It is "weak," not through any weakness in God, not through any weakness in law; it is weak "through the flesh," through the fallen and perverse nature of those over whom it seeks to extend its sway. If I go to an asylum for the insane, and preach there the gospel, the gospel is "weak," not through any weakness in itself, not, it may be, through any special weakness in my presentation of it; it is weak through the diseased condition of those to whom it is preached.

Having found, then, the cause of the limitation of the Divine law to be not in God, but in the sinfulness of the nature of man, the greatest of all questions then arises: How has God offset that limitation of which man himself is the cause? Is there anybody or anything able to do "what the law could not do"? The answer to that question makes me a Christian, not as a matter of arbitrary choice, but under the logic of necessity. After examining and sifting all the evidences, outward and inward, historical and spiritual, that bear upon the subject, I perceive that God has offset the limitation of the Divine law by three gifts, — by the gift of the Saviour to redeem; by the gift of the Spirit to renew; by the gift of the Word to enlighten.

By the gift, I say, of the Saviour to redeem. "For what the law could not do, in that it was weak through the flesh, God sending His own Son in the likeness of sinful flesh, and for sin, condemned sin in the flesh." "Christ was once offered to bear the sins of many."[1] "He is the propitiation for our sins, and not for ours only, but also for the whole world."[2] "For He hath made Him to be sin for us, Who knew no sin, that we might be made the righteousness of God in Him."[3]

God has offset the limitation of the Divine law by the gift of the Spirit to renew. "Not by works of righteousness which we have done, but according to His mercy He saved us, by the washing of regeneration and renewing of the Holy Ghost; which He shed on us abundantly through Jesus Christ our Saviour; that being justified by His grace, we should be made heirs according to the hope of eternal life."[4]

God has offset the limitation of the Divine

---

[1] Heb. ix. 28.
[2] 1 Jno. ii. 2, R. V.
[3] 2 Cor. v. 28.
[4] Tit. iii. 5–7.

law by the gift of the Word to enlighten. "Of His own will begat He us by the word of truth."[1] "Being born again, not of corruptible seed, but of incorruptible, by the word of God, which liveth and abideth forever."[2]

I find myself drawn, then, to the conviction that there are three essential things which distinguish Gospel Christianity from all other alleged forms of Christianity: The atoning Saviour is essential; the Holy Ghost is essential; the revealed Word of God is essential, — the Saviour to redeem; the Spirit to renew; the Word to enlighten. In these three essentials I find God's complete offset to the limitation of law. Redemption, renewal, enlightenment, — these are the things that the law could not do in that it was weak through the flesh. Redemption, renewal, enlightenment, — these are the hopes that lift one out of pessimism into Christianity. Redemption, renewal, enlightenment, — these are the good news of God to a blighted, hopeless world: redemption through an incarnate Saviour, renewal through a regenerating Spirit, enlightenment through an inspired Revelation of truth.

To every heart which feels the pressure of those human conditions, personal and univer-

[1] Jas. v. 18.   [2] 1 Pet. i. 23.

sal, that have driven so many into bitter, restless pessimism; which is conscious of sin in itself, and which, with a shudder of horror, conceives what sin and death are doing in the world to-day; to every such thoughtful heart God offers these truths, the only solution of the human problem for the individual or for the race. Redemption by the Saviour; renewal by the Spirit; enlightenment by the Word. And as to your own personal action in relation to these three gifts, I say: For redemption, believe, with the whole weight of a desperate faith, — believe on the Lord Jesus Christ; for renewal, submit your mind to the Holy Ghost, and go with Him where He leads; for enlightenment, reverence this Book, as the deathless Word of God; this Book, never free, since Christ came, from the attacks of infidel and rationalist; never more certain than now to stand unshaken till Christ shall come again. Amen.

IV.

THE JOYS THAT ARE PURCHASED BY SORROW.

IV.

THE JOYS THAT ARE PURCHASED BY SORROW.

"They that sow in tears shall reap in joy."—PSALM cxxvi. 5.

I DESIRE to speak of the Joys that are purchased by Sorrow. In one way or another, probably every experience of our life may be looked upon as the result of something else. Nothing comes separately and without a cause. We are perpetually tracing connections between causes and effects, either accounting for what is, or estimating what might have been, under other conditions. When our child is smitten with fever, the first thought is, "Where and when was she exposed?" When Lazarus is borne to his untimely grave, the sisters say to Christ, "If Thou hadst been here our brother had not died."

Among the things woven into the pattern of every life are sorrow and joy. Sorrow and joy are both causes and effects. Of one person we say, "Sorrow has broken down his health." Of another person we say, "Joy has made a new man of him." Here sorrow and joy are represented as causes. Again, of one we say, "He is in sorrow by reason of his mother's death," and of another, "He is full of joy because his child has come out into the light of the spiritual life." Here joy and sorrow are represented as effects resulting from these various events. In our text, joy is represented to us as an effect produced through sorrow as its antecedent. "They that sow in tears shall reap in joy." This presents to our minds the conception of joys that are purchased by sorrow. We feel this to be a profound conception, only to be understood by careful analysis. It may perhaps assist us to make this analysis, if, for the moment, we place before our minds the contrary proposition to that we are about to consider, and ask, Are there sorrows that are purchased by joy? Unquestionably there are.

This is found often to be realized in connection with the possession of great natural gifts. He who has in unusual measure the genius of music holds the passport to a world of joy whose very existence is unknown by others. To him is granted the peace, or the insight, or the aspiring courage, or the rapture, which belong to the various realms of tone; for him is the bliss of access to the palace of harmony, where, even when walking in the noisy street, or pacing the bounding deck far out at sea, he can in silent joy be mentally walking through room after room of splendor, ascending and descending golden stairs, and standing reverently before apocalyptic pictures. But he is bound to suffer; this joy will often purchase for him a pain, a restlessness, a depression, a sense of horrid discord in life, escaped by others, who, being unable to follow him to his heights, are not called to suffer with him in his depths.

The sorrow that is purchased by joy is found to be realized in connection with the finer training of the intellect. What noble happiness comes to a creature made in God's image, as he becomes conscious of intellectual growth, realizes in himself capacities more profound and powers more vigorous, conquers new departments of knowledge, and surrounds his mind with the thoughts of scholars and philosophers, as with a band of faithful and congenial friends. He knows that his critical instincts have been trained; that his opinions are more mature and more worthy; that his outlook upon the great arena of human reason and speculation is far more broad and discriminating than of old. This is joy, and yet he is bound to suffer for it, in ways from which the ignorant and the undisciplined shall never suffer. "He that increaseth knowledge increaseth sorrow."[1] The unquenchable fires of intellectual ambition must now forever burn him, and a thousand fears, doubts, and anxious reflections, to which ignorance remains a happy stranger, shall take possession of his mind.

The sorrow that is purchased by joy is realized by the intense believer in Christ. No one suffers so acutely from the bitter reproaches of a condemning conscience, no one bows himself so deeply in the dust of humiliation, as he who best knows the sweetness of the name of Jesus, and the sublimity of the new life. Other men may have been able to confess Christ without emotion, and to live in the new life without joy. He has not been able to escape the happiness; for the intensity of his belief in the risen Master has created a glorifying sense of fellowship with Him, which, amidst the commonplaces of earth, gives to life a daily gift of dignity, and freedom, and joyousness. As he goes to his common tasks, he feels that a dear Guardian is thinking of him and loving him, and often, in the sudden perplexities of life, he hears that faithful word behind him saying,

[1] Eccl. i. 18.

"This is the way."[1] And this is his joy, — a joy which, I truly think, has not its equal on earth, because it is an all-comprehending joy, that embraces with overshadowing wings every other holy joy which life contains. But he who has this joy must suffer for it. A relationship so transcendent in its spiritual import, so sensitive, so sacred, is disturbed by sins which pass unnoticed over the experience of other lives. The spiritual life becomes sensitive as the eyeball, where a grain of dust, which would be brushed unconsciously from the hand, occasions an agony that demands immediate attention and relief.

The sorrow that is purchased by joy is realized when the desolating separations of time or the dissolving touch of death bring to an end the most precious companionships of our life. Do we not know when we love intensely that this ecstatic delight of unrestrained affection is daily adding intensity to that desolation which would set in, were death to snatch away the object of our joy? Do we not understand, when we allow ourselves to become dependent upon the strong and steadfast friend, when we permit ourselves to condition our peace of mind and our exercise of choice upon the privi-

[1] Isa. xxx. 20, 21.

lege of conference with the human heart that seems to know us almost better than we know ourselves, we are storing up profounder loneliness for those years when we may call, and that friend cannot answer us, when we may seek, and that friend cannot be found? Do we not perceive that the happier a home is, that the more dear our children are, by so much shall those joys purchase larger draughts of sorrow, as the years draw nigh when all this is changed? We do know it; we do understand it; we do perceive it; yet if we are wise we will only love our treasures more tenderly, and live in our friends more richly, "while we may," assured that God has somewhere for us, here or above, full compensation for sorrows that are purchased by such pure and noble joys.

These reflections, following upon what may be called the reverse presentation of this subject, prepare our minds the more keenly to appreciate that element in the words of our text which has so greatly endeared them to human hearts. "They that sow in tears shall reap in joy." As thoughtful persons pass through life they are, as we have seen, compelled to admit that man's experience, on some of its finest and most elevated lines, is the purchase of sorrow by joy, — that the concentration of the purest happiness involves, in many ways, the possibility, if not the certainty, of more poignant sorrow. It has ever seemed, therefore, a most blessed equalizing of man's lot to be assured that life contains for some at least, if not for all, joys that are purchased by sorrow; that all which may begin in tears does not of necessity end in tears; that there are harvestings for some marvellously unlike the seed-sowings; nay, more, that there are joys which could not be the heart-filling, strength-renewing things they are, had they not sprung out of pain and the sowings of tears. The moment we set our minds upon this theme, "The joys that are purchased by sorrow," we perceive its far-reaching, manifold applications to the life and the energy of man. To say that well-nigh every joy in human life has some element or touch of sadness blended with it, is a truth, but not the truth we are endeavoring to express to-day. He who was the deepest student of the heart's joy and suffering, of life's mixed light and darkness, that has spoken since the Hebrew psalmists, has spoken of "our joys" as "three parts pain."[1] Granting that they are, this is not the thought that is chiefly embodied in that

[1] Robert Browning, *Rabbi Ben. Ezra*.

magnificent line of hope, "They that sow in tears shall reap in joy." That tells us not so much of the pain that may be mixed with joy, but of the joy that is purchased and purchasable only through pain. There is such joy, and it is the harvest of those who have been brave enough to sow in tears. Herein is a law, reaching, in its scope, from things physical and material up to things that link our nature in with the very Cross and Passion of the Son of God, — the law of joy that is purchased by sorrow.

Some are shut out from the scope of this law so that it does not cover them nor touch them; they live and die outside of its influence. Who are they that live outside of its influence? They are those who have sought happiness as an end in itself, and as the chief purpose of life, and who have set themselves to attain that end by evading pain, and strain, and the hardness of things wherever they can; they are those who have, consciously or unconsciously, confused the idea of sorrow and hardness with the idea of evil, as, in common, things to be avoided; they have confounded ease with good, and have lived, making a study of ease, calculating how to carry on life with the minimum disturbance of ease. I speak in perfect kindness and good faith when I say: "They have their reward;" such a theory of life has its obvious compensations. But such a life, with its inherent dread of discomfort, and, at last, its almost involuntary protest against sorrow, seems, I think, to be doing its own finer selfhood a perpetual injustice in making so much of ease; for it is compelling itself to live, so far as possible, outside of that broad zone of experience, and outside of that great law within which are surely comprehended some of the most truly grand manifestations of character, and some of the most truly lofty joys, which have ever been, — the joys that are purchased by sorrow.

Down, as I have said, into matters which are physical and material, and up, as I have said, into things which link our nature with the very Cross and Passion of the Son of God, reaches this broad and profoundly human law of the joys that are purchased by sorrow. "They that sow in tears shall reap in joy!" Is it not the law of the athlete, as through weeks and months he surrenders his freedom and his ease to lead, under sternest discipline, the life of hardship; and then, schooled by privation, goes into the field where pain and possible injury await him? But when the flags are waving and ten thousand sympathetic voices are telling him his victory, then he reaps in joy. Does he regret the painful sowing, the privation, the uncompromising tutelage, the sprained hand, the aching muscles, the throbbing head? No!

> "He may smile at troubles gone
> Who sets the victor-garland on!" [1]

"They that sow in tears shall reap in joy!" Is it not the law of the mountain-climber? Over the foothills and up the glen, out on the miles of bog, out on the gigantic shoulder, on toward the slippery screes — and his limbs are aching as with rheumatism, and drops like tears are falling from his face, though it is bitterly cold. But no bed of down could tempt him to stop, no flowery valley of delight could draw him back from that cold, inhospitable crag, up which, lying almost against the rugged hill, torn by a freezing wind, he is making the last grand effort. He loves the freezing wind, and the pain, and the bald, solitary crag; for here, even here at last, is the cairn, — the earth and the clouds are below him, and he reaps in joy!

"They that sow in tears shall reap in joy!"

---

[1] *St. Joseph of the Studium*, circ. A. D. 830, tr. Rev. Jno. Mason Neale.

Is it not the law of him who conquers sloth? "Yet a little sleep, a little slumber, a little folding of the hands to sleep,"[1] — so pleads the flesh, ignobly cautious of itself, daunted by base visions of shivering discomfort. But the spirit halts not at the pleading of the flesh. Taught of God, it knows how much of character ebbs away in life's minor indulgences, or is built up in the endurance of life's minor discomforts; how many greater battles are lost or won beforehand on these small, inglorious battlefields; and brushing away the webs of sloth, accepting, nay, welcoming and rejoicing in the strengthening tonic of discomfort, it saves the whole day by the sunrise victory, and reaps in joy.

"They that sow in tears shall reap in joy." Is it not the sacred law of home life? As with the years come these mystical burdens of care and grief and pain and sickness and separation; as the life of one is imperilled for another, and the toil of one is poured out for all; as the loves and solicitudes of all are twined and intertwined, and perchance as the ivies of memory are clustering over some grave that has been many times sown with tears, is there not each year a richer reaping in joy, that could not have

---

[1] Prov. xxiv. 33.

been the joy it is but for the hallowed soil of immortal experiences out of which it springs?

"They that sow in tears shall reap in joy." Is not this the law of sympathy? Oh, mistake of mistakes! to think that they are happiest who enter least into the sorrows of others; who fly, like moths, always where the light is brightest. Ah! my companions of many years, who by the loveliness of your examples have so often taught me the depth, the tenderness, the versatility of Christian sympathy, how well you know that the true sons of consolation are the happiest men on earth; that there is a joy which, like heaven's own light, descends upon one and illumines one's path, when one knows that that most holy office of the comforter has not been essayed in vain. Ah, what sympathy costs! what it takes out of one's life, when it ceases to be conventional, and becomes the true "συμπάσχω," "suffering with," only they know who have thus suffered with their fellow-men! And what it gives back to one's life, — the greater things it puts into one's soul, the reapings of joy purchased by these sowings of tears, — they only who have known the one can conceive the other!

But there is one other application of this law of the joys that are purchased by sorrow, and one only among the many which yet remain undescribed, of which I wish at this time to speak. It is one which may be truly said to link our lives with the very Cross and Passion of the Son of God. "They that sow in tears shall reap in joy." Is not this the law of all higher spiritual effort? I dare not lead you to infer from this that every spiritual effort which we make is crowned with success. That, alas! may not be true. There may be those whose life has for years been one of sad effort, to whom no joyful reaping of their heart's desire is allotted. Let us, then, draw no false or misguiding inference from these words. But let us surely catch the true thought that is here brought before the mind of every one of us who knows what spiritual effort means. "They that sow in tears shall reap in joy." They shall have the joy who have loved their work well enough to be willing to suffer in the doing of it. How many can bear witness that all the greater spiritual efforts of our lives for others must be a sowing in tears. There are reasons which, applicable to one case and to another, make it true of all that when the joy does come after spiritual effort, it is a joy purchased by sorrow. In earlier days I was surprised at this, and much disheartened that there should be so much sorrow in my work. Now I perceive it is a law, common to all the greater forms of spiritual effort, and that I could not have had the later joy of any effort without the foregoing sorrow. Why is this? In some instances the sorrow of the higher spiritual effort springs from what in the physical world would be called the resistance of matter. In the spiritual world, it is the resistance of the life or the lives for which you are pouring yourself out: sometimes an active resistance, defiant or flippant; more often a passive resistance, as of dead matter, not knowing what you mean, not caring what you mean.

Again the sorrow of the spiritual effort springs from the utter uncertainty which environs it. You have shot an arrow in the air. Where has it fallen? You have poured the very life of your life out like water on the ground. Where has it sunken out of sight?

Again, the sorrow of the spiritual effort springs from the awful sense of personal limitation: God so infinite, you so terribly finite; God's truth so sky-broad, the measure of your mind so narrow; Christ's love so mighty, your voice, proclaiming it, so feeble; till the earthen vessel of one's life seems almost to degrade and belittle the treasure committed to it.

Again, the sorrow of the spiritual effort springs from the travail of the soul. If we ourselves were not in Christ and of Christ, this would not be. We might still love with a human love, and work with a human interest for the objects nearest to us, but we would not have the travail of the soul. But this is the very signature of Jesus upon our work, showing us that, after all, it is not ours, but His. It is not we alone who are sorrowing over this wayward soul, going so fast away from God; it is not we alone who are working in an almost anguish of desire to help this mind captured by doubts, and so helpless, to make that great self-surrender to Christ. It is He, — it is He, Who is sorrowing with us, Who is working with us. When one thinks of this, one is ready to accept the sorrow of the higher spiritual effort, and to go on, sowing in tears.

But now and again Christ, Who is working with and sorrowing with one and another of us in our higher spiritual efforts, — Christ sees of the travail of His Soul and is satisfied, and that for which He and we travailed is done, — a soul is brought into the new life. Then, the joy. Ah! some of you know it. Mothers, who for their sons have sown in tears year after year; and now the joy of reaping exceeds in one day the sorrow of those years. Friends, who have sown in tears for other friends, lovely and noble in all things but that one thing, — the loveliness of Christ; and now the reaping, the coming again with rejoicing, bringing their sheaves with them.

"They that sow in tears shall reap in joy." And how little any of us can know on earth of what that means, concerning the resurrection of the blessed dead from graves that we have set with flowers and that we have watered with tears; concerning the resurrection of buried efforts, that we had mournfully laid aside as fruitless forever, but over which Christ has watched, preserving a germ that shall be revealed in heaven; concerning the resurrection of our own selfhood in that nobler life, when all the intensity of present experiences, and all the pathos of present limitations shall be changed to the glorious expression and the spiritual boundlessness of "the Life that is life indeed." Amen.

V.

THE ELEMENT OF SILENCE IN PERSONAL RELIGION.

V.

THE ELEMENT OF SILENCE IN PERSONAL RELIGION.

"A time to keep silence." — ECCLESIASTES iii. 7.

THE theme is, The Element of Silence in Personal Religion. There is a time to speak; a time for the clear, courageous word of testimony; a time when, as Peter says, we must acknowledge and justify our hope by giving with meekness and with reverence a reasonable account of it to those who ask:[1] but there also comes in every life a time to keep silence; a time when silence is more sublime, more humble, and worthier of a son of God, than speech.

When we examine the history of religious opinion, and attempt to arrange the views which have been held regarding man's relation to Divine Truth, we find two extremes, — the extreme of under-statement and the extreme of over-statement. The extreme of under-statement is Agnosticism, — that you cannot know

[1] 1 Pet. iii. 15.

anything definitely about God and life; consequently you cannot say anything definitely about God and life. The extreme of overstatement is excessive Affirmation, — that we have a full and definite revelation of God and life; consequently it is our duty definitely to affirm in words all that is revealed of God and life, for the purpose of making our system of theology complete. Granting entirely the sincerity with which both of these extreme views are held, I am certain that each view does injustice to personal religion, and that both views, though proceeding from exactly opposite standpoints, do precisely the same kind of injustice. I will explain: Here are two men; one is a Cornish miner, one is a Swiss shepherd. They meet as inmates in an asylum for the blind. The Swiss shepherd asks the Cornish miner, "How came you to be blind?" And he says, "Too much darkness. I lived in a mine; I made no allowance for light; finally my sight gave way." And the Cornish miner asks the Swiss shepherd, "How came you to be blind?" And he says, "Too much light. I lived on the snow mountains. I made no allowance for shadow, and at last my sight gave way." Now these men lived in opposite extremes of primary condition; they committed the same injustice of making no allowance for an indispensable physical compensation. They met at length in the gloom of a common calamity. So the man who embraced Agnosticism, who taught himself to affirm nothing, who made no allowance for the speech power of the immortal spirit, did, at length, the same kind of injury to his own spiritual life that was done by the man who felt it his duty to affirm in words all that may be known of God; who attempted to formulate all truth; who made no allowance for those conceptions of God which we can only know in silence, and for those agonizings and aspirings of faith and of hope which are belittled by words, which rise immeasurably above the scope of speech. The one practically denies the time to speak. The other practically denies the time to keep silence. Both are unjust to themselves. Both may unconsciously be standing in the same shadow.

I am to illustrate to-day the place and power of the element of silence in personal religion. I enter upon this effort with extreme willingness: because it is so perfectly evident to me that God is unsearchable, and that life is unsearchable: it is indeed an infinite relief to believe that I am under no obligation even to try to affirm in my words all that I seem to see revealed of God; nor even to try to explain all that I see of the movings of the Hand of God in human life. It is indeed an infinite relief to believe that I have the right to be silent, and that by this silence I do neither evade my duty, nor stultify my intelligence, nor trifle with my own sincerity.

If we may apply to this subject an argument from analogy, the duty of regarding the element of silence as a perpetual element of personal religion would seem to be powerfully suggested to our minds by the course which God sees fit to pursue in the administration of His providential government, as well as in His government of grace. How little, of all that God does, does He see fit to explain to us in our present state of existence! How constantly, in the realms of Providence and of Grace, He is apparently saying to us, "What I do thou knowest not now, but thou shalt know hereafter"![1] Perceive in the realm of Providence how life, growth, suffering, death, are inexplicable. Life! who knows its origin? For a time it was triumphantly believed that the secret of Life had been discovered in spontaneous generation. But that has been thrown

[1] St. Juo. xiii. 7.

aside, as an exploded hypothesis, by the great thinkers who proclaimed it. Professor Momerie, in his splendid book on Agnosticism, pays a well-deserved tribute to Professor Tyndall's scientific heroism in repudiating his own doctrine of spontaneous generation. "I know of nothing nobler," says Momerie, "than the conduct of Professor Tyndall in regard to the theory of spontaneous generation. He himself hoped that it would turn out true, and yet it was by his own laborious efforts that the experiments, previously supposed to have established it, were proved unsatisfactory."[1] Growth! who knows its law? "Which of you by taking thought can add one cubit to his stature?"[2] Or who can account for the process of that mystic change whereby the being which was once a helpless nursling in our arms is presently bounding at our side in youth's bravery, or bending down to us in manly tenderness to support our tottering age? Suffering! What of it? Truly we who are privileged to minister in the places of pain may note the heart-straining phenomena of Suffering, may in each specific instance assign a cause for pain; but who — ah, who! — has yet accounted for the allotments of Suf-

---

[1] Momerie's *Agnosticism*, pp. 28, 29.
[2] St. Matt. vi. 27.

fering? who has found a clue to the distribution of pain? Death! we have seen it. Ah! bethink you, have we seen it? We have seen the dying; we have seen the dead; but who has seen Death? Who has discovered what Death is? No man can explain to us Life, Growth, Suffering, Death, and when we ask of God, God answers us by silence. So does He, as well, under the government of Grace. What is that new life we call the Regeneration? How works upon our spiritual substance that Divine Regenerator, that Power-agent of the new birth? "The wind bloweth where it listeth, and thou hearest the sound thereof, but canst not tell whence it cometh and whither it goeth. So is every one that is born of the Spirit."[1] Think of this element of silence in God's natural and spiritual administrations, and reason from it to the element of silence in personal religion: it is our best, our humblest, our sublimest answer to the silence of God. Where He has not explained Himself, why need we presume it our duty to try to explain Him? Where He has disclosed Himself but dimly, why should we feel bound to affirm Him distinctly? Where He has covered Himself with darkness, why should we try to

[1] St. Jno. iii. 8.

probe Him with light? Through each crowded, throbbing year of ministry among human lives, I am brought to realize more solemnly how unsearchable God is, and how unsearchable life is. I feel more and more that, in dealing with Divine Truth and in dealing with human life, there are, for us all, times to keep silence; there are phases of God and phases of life where affirmation is not demanded, because affirmation is impossible; where explanation is not enjoined, because explanation is impracticable; there are conceptions of God only to be known in silence; there are agonies and aspirations of faith and of hope which rise above the tangled forests of words into the white, motionless mountain-peaks of silence.

Before going a step further, I wish to guard myself from being misunderstood by any. I conceive of personal religion as mainly affirmative. There is far more speech than silence in it. It abounds in gladdening, quickening, moving affirmations. I believe that the Life Eternal involves not only the power of knowing the only true God, and Jesus Christ Whom He hath sent, but the power of affirming our knowledge of God in Christ. Hear that marvellous series of affirmations with which John closes the first epistle: " He that hath the Son hath the life; he that hath not the Son of God hath not the life. These things have I written unto you, that ye may *know* that ye have eternal life. This is the boldness which we have toward Him, that if we ask anything according to His Will, He heareth us; and if we *know* that He heareth us whatsoever we ask, we *know* that we have the petitions which we have asked of Him. We *know* that whosoever is begotten of God sinneth not. We *know* that we are of God, and the whole world lieth in the Evil One. And we *know* that the Son of God is come and hath given us an understanding, that we *know* Him that is true."[1]

These are knowledges that we can express in words. But I also believe that expressible and explainable truths do not constitute all the truths we are competent to hold; that above and beyond the limits of expression sweep the fields and heights of silence; that no creed is exhaustive, — that no creed can be, because there are truths which transcend formulation, and which must be read between the lines; that I can never say all I believe; that this is not that I believe less than I say, but that I believe more and greater than I can say; that

[1] 1 Jno. v. 12–20.

there are phases of God's Being, His counsels, His decrees, His esoteric Life; and that there are phases of human experience and destiny which lie in ranges transcending human affirmation, and calling for faith and for hope, whose wings would be broken, whose breath would be stifled, by words, — whose one condition of living at such an altitude is silence.

A time to keep silence! Of the day and the hour when that time shall break in calm waves of stillness over any troubled soul knoweth no man save as the Father leads him on. There is a time when silence is the utterance of wisdom; a time when silence is the answer of power; a time when silence is the speech of faith; a time when silence is the unspeakable hope.

There is, I say, a time when silence is the utterance of wisdom. It is the time when the soul frames before itself the conception of God's eternal decrees. "Be still, and know that I am God."[1] Be still and know! Relate those words to one another; relate them as cause and effect, — Be still and know, — and they open to you a wondrous suggestion, — of knowledge, whose price is stillness, whose annihilation is the confusion, the impotence of

[1] Ps. xlvi. 10.

words. "Be still and know that I am God." Is it an injustice to the powers of language, an injustice to our own intelligence, to admit that the *modus* of God's secret consciousness transcends verbal formulation, except where God the Holy Ghost has used language in the process of revelation? Is it not rather an acknowledgment of strength than a confession of weakness, that in the endeavor to conceive of the Divine consciousness, and the Divine counsels, and the Divine decrees, we are permitted to attain, through the medium of silent communion, a conception of God superior to and more boundless than any conception which we can formulate under the inflexible forms of language? Do we not come nearer to God in thought than we can ever describe in speech? Has not the communion of the invisible soul with the Invisible God attained its highest consummations when — I will not say speech deserted us, but when we deserted speech, and climbed into the holy mount of silence, and were still, and knew that God is God? When I ask myself, "Why does our conception of God become silent as it becomes supreme?" I find no answer but that in which Paul described to the Corinthians, in faltering words, the crowning experience of his spiritual life:

"I know a man in Christ,—fourteen years ago,—such a one caught up even to the third heaven. And I know such a man, how that he was caught up into Paradise, and heard unspeakable words which it is not lawful for a man to utter."[1]

There is a time when silence is the answer of power. It is the time when controversy seeks to overthrow our personal faith in Christ. In the day when Jesus stood (even as to many He appears yet to stand) before the judgment seat of man, when He was accused by the chief priests and elders, He answered nothing. "Then saith Pilate unto Him: Hearest Thou not how many things they witness against Thee? And He gave him no answer, not even to one word, insomuch that the governor marvelled greatly."[2] Was He deaf? Did He not really hear the charges brought against Him? Or was His Soul, even in that turbulent and distressing hour, communing with His Father in that inner sanctuary of power, and girding Itself so diligently for the coming Cross He thought not of His accusers save to forgive them and to pray for them? The possibility of controversy impends over the path of every Christian; he

---

[1] 2 Cor. xii. 2–4, R. V.
[2] St. Matt. xxvii. 13, 14, R. V.

is likely at any time to have his faith assailed, his hope questioned. Nor should he purchase an ignoble peace by evading that meek and reverent answer which, alike on the lip of the scholar and of the child, is a becoming tribute to the Master. There is no intrinsic unfairness in controversy, no reason for resenting the challenge surely to be flung at us sooner or later. But there comes a stage in controversy when the effort is made to impugn and to overthrow our personal faith in Christ; when He is brought to the judgment-seat and taunted with false witness, as of old; and when we, identified with Him, are asked to reply in His stead. He has told us, by His own conduct, what to do. It is a time to keep silence. Where He no longer spoke for Himself, we need no longer speak for Him. Silence was then, silence is still, the answer of power; silence like His Own, strong, patient, self-consciously Divine. Well may they who have the witness in themselves regard life as too short, too busy, and too grand to spend, in the quibbles of controversy, strength that should be kept for work, for prayer and for suffering!

There is a time when silence is the speech of faith. It is the time when the iron of bereavement and other suffering enters into the soul. "I was dumb, I opened not my mouth, because Thou didst it." [1] This silence, which asks not why God did, but is dumb because He did it, is the highest eloquence of faith. For the instinct of suffering is to ask a reason. None who have been much with suffering can doubt that this is the instinct. The first word in the vocabulary of the deeper sorrows is, "Why?" Sometimes that word is spoken in the bitterness of a broken-hearted protest against the will of God, but far oftener as the distressing and unsatisfying question of a baffled Christian, torturing the spirit in vain efforts to assign a reason for the stroke. I thank God that faith consists neither in asking nor in answering that terrible "Why?" — that the highest speech of faith in such an hour is silence. "I was dumb because Thou didst it." Faith is in being silent when one knows not why. We only know that suffering is a part of our appointment here.

> "If, impatient, thou let slip thy cross,
> Thou wilt not find it in this world again,
> Nor in another: here, and here alone,
> Is given thee to *suffer* for God's sake.
> In other worlds we shall more perfectly
> Serve Him and love Him, praise Him, work for Him,
> Grow near and nearer Him with all delight.
> But then we shall not any more be called
> To *suffer*, which is our appointment *here*.

[1] Ps. xxxix. 9.

> "Let us take heed in time
> That God may now be glorified in us.
> And while we suffer, let us set our souls
> To suffer perfectly; since this alone,
> The suffering, which is this world's special grace,
> May here be perfected and left behind." [1]

Finally: There is a time when silence is the unspeakable hope. It is the time when the mystery of human destiny overpowers us. For some of us, life in its past, its present, and its future aspects presents such impenetrable mysteries, we see such things in our own life problems and in the problem and destiny of innumerable other beings, as drive us to the unspeakable despair or to the unspeakable hope. It is vain, it is unlawful, it is rash, it is unscriptural, it is impossible to put an unspeakable hope into words of affirmation. To affirm an unspeakable hope is to destroy it as a hope by making it an unscriptural dogma. But who could live, other than a life of strange dulness, without that unspeakable, unwritable hope: the hope that still, amidst thwarted longings and unanswered prayers, we shall yet not fail of revealing unto others the All-perfect Good, nor fail, out of hunger, to be made satisfied, out of weariness, to be made strong; the hope that they for whom we have prayed shall not

---

[1] *The Disciples*, H. E. H. King, pp. 118, 119.

perish as if we had not prayed, nor die as if we had not lived? Who shall forbid that unspeakable hope? Shall the Interceding Saviour forbid it, Whose Soul, in travail still, is one day to be satisfied?[1] Who shall forbid the unspeakable hope that, when the clouds lift and the smoke of time is blown before the clear wind of eternity, we may see that the power of the Cross has conquered in many a heart where, by all outward tokens, it seemed to have had no victory? Who shall forbid the unspeakable hope that, when the clouds lift and the smoke of time is blown before the clear wind of eternity, we may find that the agencies of the Redeeming Sacrifice have penetrated, in ways and unto depths unknown to us, into that countless throng of human intelligences who for two hundred generations have been swept into eternity with no human voice to tell them that Jesus is the Redeemer, slain from the foundation of the world,[2] and that His Blood cleanseth us from all sin?[3] Amen.

[1] Isa. liii. 11.   [2] Rev. xiii. 8.   [3] 1 Jno. i. 7.

VI.
THE MINISTRY OF CHANGES.

VI.

THE MINISTRY OF CHANGES.

"Because they have no changes, therefore they fear not God." — PSALM lv. 19.

I WOULD speak of the *Ministry of Changes*. The verse of which the text is a part is ranked by Hebraists as one of the obscure verses of God's Word. Ewald, Hengstenberg, Perowne, and Thrupp are in opposition to one another regarding the meaning of the Psalmist: but I can find from them and from others nothing clearer or more probable than the rendering in our own Common Version, and that rendering contains a truth so searching and so suggestive, I take the reading in the Common Version just as it stands: "Because they have no changes, therefore they fear not God."

When we look upon the life of a community for any considerable period of time, we discover very great differences in the allotment of life's serious and trying changes. Three types of experience present themselves. We see some individuals and some households which during this long period are exempt from all serious and saddening change: the tide of peaceful prosperity is one long flood with no ebb; the main conditions of living appear established on foundations that cannot be shaken; year follows year in tranquil succession; and we say, "They are not in trouble like other men." But at their very side, all these years, have been persons and households tried with the discipline of incessant changes: almost no element of their life has been untouched by the alterations of time; almost no quiet spaces of permanence have been granted unto them; their life has been transitional, experimental, irregular. Between these two extreme types is a third: the home that through the greater part of this period has been sheltered from changes; has enjoyed a rich measure of that blessed and bountiful sameness. But now it has had not many changes; perhaps only one or two: and oh, how they have altered the meaning of life! One dear lamb has been taken out of the fold; but how that single going forth has changed all! One dear-friend influence has vanished out of the daily life; but how many things have lost the touch of that light-giving friend!

It is true there are many changes coming

upon us, in the bounty of God, which are always and only happy. Every sunrise is a change; every new year; every new voice; every new friend; every new power is a change.

> "New every morning is the Love
> Our wakening and uprising prove.
> New mercies each returning day
> Hover around us as we pray."

Yes, the multiplyings of our precious things are changes: but it is not of these changes I speak to-day; not of the gifts we gain, but of the gifts we lose; not of the changes that make our life more full and more complete, but of those that leave it emptier; of those that take out of it joys long delighted in, help long relied upon; of those that in their occurrence shatter familiar conditions, and force the soul forth into untried and undesired pilgrimage; of those that show us our own weakness, and compel us trembling to begin again the great experiment of living.

The thought of changes is to most of us a sad thought. To some, more than to others, it is a most bitter thought; for some natures, more than others, depend upon and delight in the unchanged continuance of every dear and treasured influence and possession. There are undoubted vestiges of the nomadic spirit in some hearts, by which it becomes easy for them to submit to great changes, — to strike their tent here to-day and pitch it far yonder to-morrow; to leave old friends and gather new ones. But other hearts strike deep roots into all that they love, and bind with strong, living ties familiar blessings; and there are some hearts that have bled to death in changes, for their clinging affections were, like arteries, full with the heart's blood. To most of us, therefore, I believe the thought of changes is a sad thought. There are reasons for this.

We depend on that which is. The vine is planted at the root of the cedar-tree, and though, had there been no tree, it might have found a fence to climb upon, or it might have wandered in the grass, it now appropriates what is, and hangs its life upon it. It wreathes that strong stem with clinging arms; it multiplies itself amidst the branches; it crowns the cedar-top in autumn with a flaming diadem of scarlet and gold. So we appropriate what is, and grow upon it. And although, had the providential conditions of our life been other than they are, we should never have understood our lack of these, it is true that God has given us these and we have clung to them, we have grown upon them, we have been upheld and uplifted by them, we have expressed and completed ourselves by means of them.

The thought of changes is sad because we grow established in a satisfying routine. We are working hard, but in work we love; we have many duties, but we have learned them, have arranged them, and familiarity has made them dear; our loved ones have brought us added cares, but their daily affection is more than compensation, and the routine of life grows satisfying. It is blessed to know well and to be well known. Established methods; home customs made easy by unnumbered repetitions; friends whose very weaknesses have grown with time not only tolerable but precious, — these make up the dear routine across which the thought of changes falls like the mournful shadow of a cloud.

The thought of changes is sad because we lean on that which gives happiness. We love the real makers of our happiness. Dependence upon existing sources of happiness is the first intuition of the heart; and by as much as the greatness of happiness is, by so much are the terror and dismay of the heart, under the thought of change. How strong yet how pathetic is the instinct to banish the thought of changes when the fountains of joy are brimful! If the wish of a happy heart could make the sun stand still, late indeed would have been the sunset on some days that we remember.

And yet, though this our first thought is so true, though the thought of changes is a sad thought, it is equally true that the absence of great changes is a condition of spiritual danger. "Because they have no changes, therefore they fear not God." There is a ministry in changes, — a ministry of grace, which He Who changes not would work in us; and they who have no changes must lose that ministry, and do in fact encounter perils in their spiritual life. Some lives are wonderfully protected from the great, heart-burdening changes which are heaped upon others. For long periods of years "they are not in trouble as other men;" their home life is singularly tranquil; their nest is not stirred; they escape the cross. This immunity from changes brings certain spiritual perils. And while I do not say that all who have no changes are overcome by these perils, yet all such are subject to them, and should be warned against them. Where the life of an individual, or the life of a family, glides on for a long, long time without any severe changes, the serene sameness of prosperity brings these dangers: First, The under-valuation of truth. Unbroken prosperity in personal or in family life tends toward the under-valuation of truth. I have sometimes seen truly strong and varied landscapes that became flat and tame in unbroken sunlight. I know some hills whose beauty I never understood except on days of many cloud-shadows. And when we remember that the gospel of salvation is a story of pain, we need not wonder if our life should need the great cloud-shadows to make us see the grandeur of Calvary. To him who has suffered as a Christian, the sufferings of Christ no longer lack meaning; to him who has submitted in meekness to the severity of changes, the Saviour's grand renunciation of Himself grows terribly and gloriously real. The peril of prosperity is deadness and dulness toward truth; hearing as though one heard not; seeing as though one saw not; handling and tasting the bread and wine of truth as though no consecrating Hands were offering them to us, no Word Incarnate saying of them: They are My Body and My Blood.

Another peril which comes in the absence of changes is the decay of gratitude. They to whom life has long been rich and full, and sheltered from impoverishing changes, are in danger of losing that blessed grace of gratefulness which sanctifies the joy of possession. We often speak of those who are hardened by adversity: are there not as often those who are hardened and alienated from the life of God, and from the proper appreciation of His gifts, by prolonged, changeless prosperity? And in speaking of prosperity, I do not only mean great financial abundance, but also the prolonged enjoyment of other and simpler things which have yet more to do with the completeness of life. Such is the gift of health, when whole years have passed without one hour of prostration or of pain; when the sense of bodily limitation is forgotten in the pride of vitality. Such also is the gift of home life, when the circle is unbroken, when no heart-rending separations have occurred to test the intensity of love; when a man begins to feel home life less wonderful and more customary. Such also is the gift of religious opportunity, when church-going becomes a habit, prayer a form, and (I must dare to say it) the Holy Communion conventional. These are some of the circumstances in which, from many a heart blessed with them through long, unchanging years, gratitude has decayed and fallen away. One may have his church so abundantly, his home so familiarly, his health so confidently, that all conception of these things as gifts of God may fade from him. "Because he has no changes, he fears not God."

Another peril, and a greater one, which comes in the absence of changes, is the loss of the sense of dependence. In the 10th Psalm a description is given of one who fears not God; and one aspect of his character is the absence of the sense of dependence. "He hath said in his heart, I shall not be moved; for I shall never be in adversity." [1] Into many a life has crept that most subtle and most terrible loss, in times of unbroken, unchanged happiness, — the loss of the sense of dependence. It has affected the soul's judgment concerning earthly things; it has undermined its earnestness in prayer; it has tempted it to intrust life to the guidance of its own sagacity, rather than to the guidance of the Spirit and the Providence of God. This soul, deceived by its own apparently established prosperity, by its own firm hold on the hearts of friends, whispers confidently to itself: "I shall never be moved, for I shall never be in adversity." It forgets that it is but a child, and

[1] Ps. x. 6.

less than a child, under the irresistible sweep of God's Will, — that He is able with one breath to blow away the established constructions of years, to melt the bands that hold friends together.

There is a degree yet deeper in which the sense of dependence has been lost through prolonged prosperity. The sense of dependence upon Christ as the only Refuge of the soul may readily be imperilled by conditions of long, unchanged success. The success of life fosters at length a spiritual self-confidence. A good reputation, acknowledged influence, the favor and friendship of the powerful, — these things may bring upon any of us the sin of Laodicea : " Because thou sayest I am rich, and increased with goods, and have need of nothing, and knowest not that thou art wretched and miserable and poor and blind and naked, I counsel thee to buy of Me gold tried in the fire, that thou mayest be rich, and white raiment, that thou mayest be clothed ; and anoint thine eyes with eye salve, that thou mayest see." [1] There are many who need these words; many whose steady and prolonged success in earthly things has built up beneath them a complaisant self-righteousness which resents the idea of being

[1] Rev. iii. 17, 18.

called a helpless and lost sinner, depending wholly for salvation on the Blood of the Son of God.

"Because they have no changes, therefore they fear not God." There is another thought in these words which we cannot state without remembering how constantly men try to forget it. The only thing perfectly certain in life is its changefulness. The law of changes is a law that cannot change. It has already been carried out in every life that has ever lived on earth; it shall be carried out to the letter in our lives. Those who seem, as we look back over the last few years, to have had many changes, are not the subjects of any peculiar law; those who seem, as we look back over the same period, to have had no changes, or almost none, have escaped the operation of this same law only for a season. If any one has built, upon the record of a few unbroken years, a theory of going on thus always, — has whispered confidently to himself, as he marked the vicissitudes of others, "I shall never be moved," — he is altogether mistaken. For the only thing certain in life is that it will change. The changes will come to each of us, as they have already come and are coming to so many of us. The firmest home that ever was built must be shaken some time: the dearest circle that ever was formed must be broken some time; the strongest health that ever was given must fail some time; the most precious work that ever was done must end some time. You cannot keep it out by love, by will, by law, by stratagem, by prayer. Life is change, — death is change. Only ONE can say, "I change not," and He is the Lord.[1]

What, then, is the meaning, what is the ministry, of our changes, these which are coming to us now, — to some slowly, to some swiftly, — in some homes many small changes, in other homes one or two great changes, which themselves have changed all? I answer, the ministry of changes is in part this: To widen our view; to deepen our humility; to intensify our trust; to bring us to present action.

The ministry of changes is to widen our view. "There is that scattereth, and yet increaseth."[2] What a wonderful wideness of meaning in those words when we apply them to some of life's changes! Here is a home that long was unbroken, but now one has gone afar into the Paradise of God. Has there been no increasing from that scattering? Though life is sadder, is it not also wider, — wider in the

[1] Mal. iii. 6.   [2] Prov. xi. 24.

region of its affection, wider in the scope of its faith, wider in the reach of its hope? Oh, who can tell the number of those whose thoughts, whose purpose, whose whole spirit, have been immeasurably widened by the discipline of changes! How often the shattering of a human plan has set a soul free in some wider plan of God!

The ministry of changes is to deepen our humility. To a proud spirit, the intrusive absoluteness of many changes is most humiliating. There are few things we grow so proud of as our power to plan adroitly and to reach foreseen conclusions. And when one of God's great, calm, resistless plans comes sweeping silently along like a noiseless wind, and sets our little plans aside like wreaths of dust, the pride of the natural heart is sorely chastised. But did we not need it? Was our heart like the heart of a little child? Were we in sympathy, before this discipline, with Him who said: "Not My Will, but Thine, be done"?[1]

The ministry of changes is to intensify our trust. Think not God chastises our pride for the sake of chastising it, — breaks in upon our plans with the great hammer-strokes of His changes only to cover us with the dust of

[1] St. Luke xxii. 42.

humiliation. God's changes look beyond the humbling of one's heart to the trust that is learned in humility. They only know what true calmness is, who, through the contravention of cherished plans, and through the humiliation of confident endeavors, and through the intrusion of startling changes, have learned the infiniteness of God's power, and have placed their lives in God's Hand, waiting now for direction.

The ministry of changes is to bring us to present action. Now or never! Much of life's sweetest, best opportunity is thus bounded. Is there love to be given? give it now! Is there wrong to be forgiven? forgive it now! Is there faith to be confessed? confess it now! Is there work of Christ-like ministry to be done? do it now! Work on in the To-day, for by To-morrow much may have changed, and changed forever. Amen.

VII.

THE EMBRACE OF GOD.

VII.

THE EMBRACE OF GOD.

"And underneath are the Everlasting Arms." — DEUT. xxxiii. 27.

OUR theme is, The Embrace of God. Not that we may and must take hold of God, but that God does take hold of us. Underneath — underneath all that makes up for us the activity of life; underneath its faith and its fear; underneath its best work and its poorest work; underneath its fitful courage and its frequent dread, — underneath all are the Everlasting Arms. The Embrace of God is deeper than our depths; when the Everlasting Arms take hold of us, they hold all that we are; they supply all that we are not.

That we may and must take hold of God, is true, yet only half the truth; that we must ever be stretching out the hands of prayer and the hands of faith, to lay hold of "the life that is life indeed," to touch and handle and hold things unseen, is true, yet only half the truth. The stronger half is the Embrace of God, and underneath, even underneath our trying to take hold of God, are the Everlasting Arms. The highest form of faith is understanding how to rest in God. The ultimate thing in a complete life is not doing but resting: there must be doing, and always doing; yet doing is not ultimate, for underneath (whether it be doing or suffering) are the Everlasting Arms. To feel this is to know our portion in God through our Lord Jesus Christ.

There is everything in the present age to make us forget this, the best thing about our life. The present age (and no doubt rightly) sets a premium upon doing. "What can you do?" "What have you done?" "What are you doing?" "What are you going to do?" These are the four questions that are the four gospels of modern secularism.

What can you do? Judge a man by his abilities: Can he hold his own? Can he compete with his fellows?

What have you done? Judge a man by his record: Has he held his own? Has he given the ring of the true metal when struck in the fight by the blows of difficulty? Has he revealed power for regular work, and skill for emergency?

What are you doing? Judge a man by his occupation: Is his work good? Is he doing high-class service? Is he industrious?

What are you going to do? Judge a man by his plans: Has he foresight? Is he visionary? Is he ambitious?

These are the four gospels of modern secularism. Each sets a premium upon doing; and in many things it is wise and safe to set a premium on doing, and to judge men by their ability, by their record, by their occupation, and by their plans. If good work is to be well done, doers have to be sifted by stern tests.

And quite right, too, that in the Christian life a premium should be set on doing, as most certainly is the case to-day. Never has that bugle-call, which summons us to our work, rung more loudly through the Church than it rings to-day. Imperatively does Christ, the Great Worker, say, "Follow Me;" and most enthusiastically is His command echoed by His under-officers down the ranks. Work is preached from all pulpits; work is animating all Christian bodies, and cementing the alliance of denominations; work, in new forms, is attracting new workers who were never workers before. I sometimes ask myself, Is work being deified just now? Is the Church making this age the apotheosis of work? For it is commended as a cure for almost all spiritual ills. It is urged as a remedy for faltering faith: if your mind is tormented with doubts, just throw yourself into work and your doubts will leave you. It is urged as a protection against sin: if you are tempted of the Devil, just fill your life with work, and you will have no time left to attend to his solicitations. It is commended as a relief from sorrow: if you are greatly afflicted, do not remain in morbid inactivity; work, and in doing for others you shall be lifted above yourself. All true! All true! Nobly, blessedly true. Christ's truth, every word of it. Yet, after all, only half the truth, and not enough without the other half. Work seems all-sufficient because there is so much of it, and of such noble kinds. "Doing" seems everything, because there are so many doing, and doing with all their might, for love of the Lord Jesus. But work is not all-sufficient, and doing is not everything; and many who work, work with heavy hearts, and do with trembling and uncertain spirit, needing and craving more than work to save them from their fears, — more than doing to make them brave. Work cannot do everything for us, for the reason that our work is so imperfect, and that it does not meet all of our needs. Doing — the stretching out of our hands to take hold of God — is not enough for us, for the reason there are so many things in our life, behind us and before us, which we cannot touch with our hands, nor see with our eyes. What we do need, beyond our doing, beyond our taking hold of God, is to feel that God has taken hold of us, and underneath are the Everlasting Arms. Our life is so full of startling wideness, of terrifying indefiniteness, of large incompleteness, the only one thing that can go under its depth, and that can encircle its breadth, and that can hold up all strongly together, is the Embrace of God!

The Everlasting Arms! What conceptions of God in relation to our lives are here given to us? To speak of the Arms of God is not to run any risk of narrowing or materializing our thought of God by the littleness of human ideas. It is a principle of inspired language, which we may follow through the whole Bible, to speak of the attributes of God by illustrations drawn from human life and human things. We do not infer at all from this that God is only such an one as ourselves, but we use these human illustrations by looking through them to bring God near to our power of thought, as the astronomer uses on earth his telescope to bring the stars near to his power of vision. See how these telescopes are mounted in the observatory of the Word: "Like as a father pitieth his children, so the Lord pitieth them that fear Him." [1] How near to our power of thought that brings God's compassion. "As one whom his mother comforteth, so will I comfort you." [2] What a strong lens that is! So, also, parts and features of the body are freely used to interpret, according to the power of our minds, the transcendent attributes of God. So, the Eyes of God,[3] the Mouth of God,[4] the Voice of God,[5] the Breath of God,[6] the Hand of God,[7] the Feet of God,[8] are all of them inspired illustrations of Divine attributes, which for the spiritual mind have no tendency to materialize the thought of God, but to bring the glorious realities of His Being within the immediate range of our powers of feeling and of faith. And thus we are told to-day, "in the blessing wherewith Moses the man of God blessed the children of Israel before his death," of the Everlasting Arms. Were there time for

---

[1] Ps. ciii. 13.
[2] Isa. lxvi. 13.
[3] Ps. xxxiii. 18.
[4] St. Matt. iv. 4.
[5] Ps. xxix. 3, 4, 5, 7, 8, 9.
[6] Job. xxxiii. 4.
[7] Isa. xxvi. 11.
[8] Eph. i. 22.

such a study, it would be a precious thing to take this oft-repeated thought of the Arm or the Arms of God, and trace out its meaning through the many Scriptures wherein it appears. We should find out how the writers of Israel loved to use that strong word, "the stretched-out Arm,"[1] as a sign of God's active help extended to His own people. We should find Hezekiah strengthening his people's heart against the invading Assyrian with this grand cry: "With him is an arm of flesh, but with us is the Lord our God to help us and to fight our battles."[2] We should find the mystic whirlwind voice saying reprovingly to Job, "Hast thou an arm like God?"[3] and the Psalmist singing joyfully: "Thou hast with thine Arm redeemed Thy people,"[4] "Thou hast scattered Thine enemies with Thy Strong Arm."[5] "His Right Hand and His Holy Arm hath gotten Him the victory,"[6] and in the Song of Solomon this wonderful prayer: "Set me as a seal upon Thine Arm, for love is strong as death."[7] And Isaiah is full of this thought. Now he prays: "Be Thou their Arm every morning;"

---

[1] Ex. vi. 6; Deut. iv. 34; 2 Chron. vi. 32; Ezek. xx. 33.
[2] 2 Chron. xxxii. 8.   [3] Job. xl. 9.
[4] Ps. lxxvii. 15.   [5] Ps. lxxxix. 10.
[6] Ps. xcviii. 1.   [7] Cant. viii. 6.

our salvation also in the time of trouble."[1] Now he asks sadly: "To whom is the Arm of the Lord revealed?"[2] Now he speaks in the words of Jehovah: "Mine Arms shall judge the people, and on mine Arm shall they trust."[3] And now he utters that most tender Messianic prophecy: "He shall gather the lambs with His Arm and carry them in His Bosom."[4] And when we turn from these few examples to the noble assurance given by Moses, "The Eternal God is thy Refuge, and underneath are the Everlasting Arms," we feel that the thought of the Arms of God is very full of meaning, that it gives us a most soul-restoring idea of the enfolding of our life in the Embrace of the Divine Life; of the strength of God's Embrace; of the protection of God's Embrace; of the permanence of God's Embrace.

The first thing that appeals to us is the strength of those Everlasting Arms: "Trust ye in the Lord forever, for in the Lord Jehovah is everlasting STRENGTH."[5] Many of us are so constituted that we depend upon the strength of some other life for our strength. We feel our need, in the earthly companion-

---

[1] Isa. xxxiii. 2.   [2] Isa. liii. 1.
[3] Isa. li. 5.   [4] Isa. xl. 11.
[5] Isa. xxvi. 4.

ship, of a strong arm to lean upon. We search the countenance of another to see if it is calm or anxious; we probe the thought of another to find if it is still brave, and so long as we find strength there we can be strong. Strength is mysteriously communicable. Some have power by a word, by a look, by a touch of the hand, to say to another, "Receive thou strength." All such, whether giving or receiving strength in present earthly companionship, can feel the strength of these Everlasting Arms. And who can more truly feel it than those from whom the strong earthly arm has been or is soon to be withdrawn? The intenser sense of dependence prepares one to appreciate the strength of these Everlasting Arms.

The next thing that appeals to us is the protection afforded by these Everlasting Arms, to all who are in their Embrace. "Hold Thou me up, and I shall be safe."[1] Life is dangerous, life is untried, life is menaced by evil. "Hold Thou me up, and I shall be safe." It is a glorious thought, that perfect safety within the Embrace of God. "Thou hast scattered Thine enemies with Thy strong Arm; Thou hast with Thine Arm redeemed Thy people."[2]

[1] Ps. cxix. 117.   [2] Ps. lxxxix. 10; lxxvii. 15.

Have not moments come to you when the sense of defencelessness has overwhelmed you? On the verge of new undertakings, whose results are deeply hidden from you; or entrusted with responsibilities where mistake may mean ruin; or bereft of counsellors on whose guidance you have been wont to depend; or plunged in peril where human aid is unavailing, — how shattering is the thought of your defencelessness! Yet in such a moment, to one who believes, there may be born within the soul a consciousness, before unknown, of the protection of those Everlasting Arms, —

> "And hearts are brave again,
> And arms are strong."

The next thing that appeals to us is the permanence, both for strength and for protection, of those Everlasting Arms. "I will never leave thee nor forsake thee."[1] How those words shine on ahead of us as we go, — a "searchlight," cutting through the fog, not revealing the path in the sea, but making the air light! The everlastingness of those strong protecting Arms is the answer to the prayer, "O Thou Who changest not, abide with me."

One thought beyond this: "*Underneath*

[1] Heb. xiii. 5.

are the Everlasting Arms." I rejoice in that "underneath." It has finality in it. It has ultimateness in it. It touches bottom, — deeper than the depths. Arthur Hallam said: "Pain is the deepest thing we have in our nature."[1] And it is true. Pain is the deepest thing we have in our nature; but there is something deeper than pain, for there is something deeper than our nature: "*Underneath* are the Everlasting Arms." And, as we close this sermon, I want to show you how this underneath thought helps our faith, how it helps our work, how it helps our courage.

How does it help our faith? Underneath our faith are the Everlasting Arms of God's covenant love in Christ. What must I do to be saved? Believe on the Lord Jesus Christ, and thou shalt be saved. Now what is the strong thing here, — my faith or God's covenant, "Thou shalt be saved"? Ah! the strength is in the Everlasting Arms of that covenant of Eternal Love which are under me in the work of Christ. My faith is a most weak, unsteady force. There are times when it grows stronger and brighter under the power of favorable influences, when I see clearly my part in the sacrifice of the Redeemer, and lay

[1] *Remains in Verse and Prose of Arthur Henry Hallam*, p. 281.

hold of His Cross with strong hands. But there are other times when the power of faith languishes, when the faults and follies of my weaker nature hinder its free exercise, and when discouragement dims its clearness. Does my salvation depend on my faith keeping up to a certain pitch of intensity? If so, where am I before God to-day, and where is my hope? Is the strength of my faith my refuge? It is not so. "The Eternal God is thy Refuge, and underneath are the Everlasting Arms." The great thing is, not the strength with which you have taken hold of God, but the strength with which God has taken hold of you, to hold you eternally in the Everlasting Arms of His covenant love revealed in Christ. The most trembling, weeping, uncertain, troubled faith, if only it be real as far as it goes, is just as truly the gateway of salvation, to the soul that has it, as is the triumphant, cloudless, untroubled faith of the greatest apostle, for the measure of faith in neither case is the ground of salvation. The ground of salvation for both alike, the ultimate fact, is that underneath the faith, be it weaker or stronger, are the Everlasting Arms of the Covenant of the Cross. If this were realized more clearly than it is, what a magnificent help it would be to the faith of all of us! We should cease feeling the pulse of our spiritual emotions, and should rest in the covenant of Calvary; and no man can feel that the everlasting, outstretched Arms of the dying Saviour are the support beneath his life without being quickened into a strong faith, and moved by a desire for holiness.

Underneath are the Everlasting Arms! How does this help our work? Underneath our imperfect work are the Everlasting Arms of Christ's perfect work. Christ's work sanctifies and makes acceptable in God's sight all work wrought, however imperfectly, in His Name. Christ's work gathers and holds our imperfect efforts in the embrace of a Divine acceptance. "Inasmuch as ye have done it unto one of the least of these my brethren, ye have done it unto Me."[1] "Unto Me"—those two words are the Everlasting Arms that gather and bind our life work, and bear it up acceptably before the Throne. Unto Me! Take away those words and our life becomes an unbound sheaf; it falls apart into scattered, frail, faulty, often futile efforts. Judged in themselves alone by the awful standard of God's Perfection, our miserable attempts at service fill us with shame.

[1] St. Matt. xxv. 40.

But is this our destiny, to go wearily on, our life marked behind us by the broken efforts that have fallen to the ground? Christian brother, this is not our destiny. No sincere work, however faulty, falls to the ground, for underneath are the Everlasting Arms, — those gracious, compassionate, gathering, and binding Arms — "Unto Me" — wherewith Christ gathers our work, enfolds it in His Own, presents it with His Own. Who that believes this but must often work with a less uncertain spirit, knowing that his labor in the Lord is not in vain; not that we have taken hold of God by our work, but that God has taken hold of our work with the Everlasting Arms?

Underneath are the Everlasting Arms! How does this help our courage? Underneath our failing heart are the Everlasting Arms of the Reserve Power in God. Can any one be truly strong who has not been perfectly weak? I mean, can any one say with truth that he knows something of the Reserve Power of those Everlasting Arms until, under the pressure of temptation, or of care, or of sorrow, he has felt the life giving way beneath him, — the flesh and the heart failing? But if you have come to that point where you felt life giving way under you, and if at that point you, with a perfect consciousness of your entire weakness, did throw the whole weight of your heavy heart upon God, then you may have known something of the Reserve Power of those Everlasting Arms that caught you and held you, and made you stronger than the strong. Courage? It is a pretty thing to look at when the bright, unburdened soul speaks out of the fearless eyes which never yet were dimmed by life's real sorrows; it is a sweet, and spring-like thing to see the impassioned courage of the boyhood that has had no reason yet to doubt itself. But it is a diviner thing to see the New Transfiguring Courage that is found in that hour when the soul, in utter weakness, flings itself on the Reserve Power of those Everlasting Arms, and grows stronger than the strong. These are the strength-givers; these are they who have grace to make others brave, who themselves out of weakness were made strong in the Embrace of God. Amen.

VIII.

THE PERSPECTIVE OF RIGHT LIVING.

VIII.

THE PERSPECTIVE OF RIGHT LIVING.

" And he looked up, and said : I see men as trees, walking."
—St. Mark viii. 23.

Here was a case for an oculist. When Cheselden, the great English eye-surgeon, first gave sight to a young man born blind, by an operation celebrated alike in the annals of surgery and psychology, the patient is said to have declared that all objects, near and distant, seemed to touch his eyes. He had no sense of distance, no perception of relations, no idea of perspective, no conception of an horizon.[1] This, substantially, was the case of the man brought to Christ at Bethsaida, for the healing of blindness. Anticipating, I doubt not, the confusion which would attend the first effort of vision, the Saviour, before operating upon the man, takes him by the hand and leads him out of the town into the quieter country-side, where, possibly, the only spectators of the cure

[1] Vide *Weekly London Times*, June 13, 1890, p. 12.

would be the disciples. Then, by a touch, He breaks the spell of blindness, and summons this child of involuntary darkness to make his first report of light. Christ laid His hands upon him and asked him: "Seest thou aught?" The man looked up, endeavored in the first bewildered exercise of a new sense to grasp the situation, and replied: "I see men as trees, walking." His reply reminds us of Cheselden's patient. He saw; but he saw not things in right relations; the near and the distant, the great and the small were all alike to him. Everything seemed to touch his eyes. He had not as yet acquired that sense of distance, that sense of perspective which is in fact the result of experience, although we may think of it as innate. I am seated upon my piazza on a summer day. Before me is a table. On the table is a book. On the same plane as the table my eye beholds the bright blue sea. On the sea is a great sloop-yacht with her clouds of snowy canvas. I stretch out my hand to touch the book. Why do I not stretch out my hand to touch the yacht, which is just beyond the book in the plane of vision? Because experience has taught my eyes the sense of perspective, of nearness and of distance, of relative sizes and positions; and I know the book is small and is near; and although the yacht appears just beyond the book and of the same size as the book, the acquired sense of perspective assures me the yacht is large and is far away.

This man, who at the bidding of that Divine Oculist, Jesus Christ, made his first effort of vision, revealed instantly that the sense of perspective is not innate, but is acquired. He declared, "I see men as trees, walking." By this he meant that he detected objects, but not their relations. Men looked like trees, trees like men. The Lord at his side and the sycamore in the meadow were simply two discernible objects, equally near, of equal size. I suppose this is the way the world looks to a baby when first it opens its eyes. The form of its father is as tall as the elm-tree, and the canopy of its crib is as high as the sky; the night-light is as bright as the sun, and the mother's hymn is as loud as the noise of trumpets. Day by day, month by month, it acquires the sense of relativeness, in sights, in sounds; the perspective of the eye, the perspective of the ear. If our Lord had done nothing further for the man beyond enabling him to make this first effort of vision wherein he saw men as trees walking, the man, proceeding along the ordinary path of human experience, could painfully and perilously have succeeded ultimately in learning the relations of objects to one another; he could have acquired his perspective. Like a baby learning the uses of eyes, gradually he would have found out that trees are taller than men; that a rod is shorter than a mile; that the sky is higher than a roof. But we are all glad to learn that Jesus by His own personal power kindly enabled this man to anticipate the slow results of experience; gave him not only vision, but the sense of perspective; for we read: "Then again He laid His hands upon his eyes; and he looked steadfastly and was restored, and saw all things clearly." [1]

It would be difficult, I think, to give even a few moments of thought to this incident, without perceiving that in it we have a suggestion concerning life of even more than ordinary power. It seems hardly possible to think of the dim, bewildered way in which the man began to use his eyes, of the confusion of men and trees, of the lack of altitude, the lack of spacing, the lack of scale, and not to think how we, when we began to look on life, may have seen it in the same dim, bewildered way, without altitude, without spacing, without scale, without perspective. It seems hardly possible to

[1] Revised Version.

think of Jesus giving this man his perspective; setting things right before his eyes; putting objects in relation, and saving him a thousand mortifications, miscalculations, blows and falls, — and not to think that Jesus has power to give us the perspective of right living, — to set things right before our eyes; to set the great sun-crowned mountains of hope and the sky-spaces of glory above the roadside bushes and above the dusty figures of men.

The perspective of right living! It is of this I would speak to-day, if God shall give me utterance. First, of the tendency to false perspective. Second, of the evils of false perspective. Third, of the Touch that makes all things clear.

"I see men as trees, walking." The tendency to false perspective is revealed in the first effort of vision. In his first report of light, the man ingenuously reports that he has everything to learn. Such seeing is hardly an advance on blindness. Such light is darkness. To detect objects without sense of relative size and place is to multiply, not to abate, the perils of existence. The blind man tapping warily along the pavement is safer than he who sees the vehicles, but knows not if they be far or near. Vision without true perspective is open-eyed blindness. Yet we tend to this when we begin to look upon life. Each in his own way, and after his own kind, tends to false perspective, and sees men as trees walking.

"I see men as trees, walking." To begin by citing an obvious example. Some tend to false perspective in the care of health. "I believe in the sanity of the body" is not a clause from the Apostles' Creed, but is worthy to be there. A man has his life-work: a woman has hers. The glory of the calling and the strength of the called were meant to correspond. "As thy days so shall thy strength be,"[1] means (as much as anything) health for a life-work. Yet nothing is more likely, than health, to stand in false perspective at the beginning of life. It is offered up ruthlessly as fuel to feed the fires of indulgence. It is diminished by the playful bravado of imprudence; by deficient sanitation of the body; by late and irregular hours; by foolish and indefensible habits. Fashion levies a pitiless and utterly exorbitant tax upon the vitality of the young, and self-indulgence coöperates with her to set the whole subject of health in false perspective. There are times when my sense of this false perspective prevailing among the young on the subject of health

[1] Deut. xxxiii. 25.

becomes so intense, it seems as if it would drag me from my pulpit and send me forth as an evangelist to schools and colleges, to preach a larger doctrine of life to boys and girls, to preach the glory and the strain of a man's life-work, and of a woman's life-work; to preach that fatherhood need not be a crushing care, nor motherhood a shattering torture; to plead for youth, as Elisha prayed for the young man in the vale of Dothan: "Open his eyes, that he may see;"[1] to sweep away the clouds of tobacco smoke from the brains of boys, to stop incipient drinking; to make girls content with simpler living; to set health in true perspective before it has been sold for pleasure.

"I see men as trees, walking." So some tend to false perspective in mental culture. It is the fashion of this age to read books. But mental culture is no more measured by the number of books one reads, than health is measured by the number of pounds one weighs. Mental culture is the process of thought-life. Thought gives perspective to knowledge. To devour books presupposes no certain thought-life. In the mass of rapidly acquired information there may be no altitude, no spacing, no scale. The near and the distant, the great and

[1] 2 Kings vi. 17.

the petty, may look alike — men as trees walking. Thought, and only thought, gives perspective to knowledge: places the data of information in right relations, informs the mind with the sense of greatness, invests mental judgments with dignity, and pervades character with calm and beauteous self-confidence. In the crowded life which many of us are compelled to live, the great foe of thought is incident, perpetual, ubiquitous incident; something to happen every hour. Incident is in the towering majority. Its tendency is to throw thought into false perspective, to minimize meditation, thus to pauperize the mind. Is there anything in the universe of God more beautiful, more desirable, than a thoughtful mind, in which, as on the face of some magnificent landscape, the lines of pure perspective are drawn by the Hand of God; where the elements of knowledge stand in right relations; where the foreground detail neither hides nor belittles the sky-line and the peaks that pierce the blue.

"I see men as trees, walking." So some tend to false perspective in the moral life. To do evil that good may come is the logic of the devil. In deliberative assemblies, occasions sometimes arise calling for unusual methods of procedure; and where the occasion is supposed to justify, the unusual procedure is allowed, under what is called "a suspension of the rules." In the life of men, how often is the moral law violated under (what a man persuades himself to believe) is a justifiable suspension of the rules. The opportunities of gain are very unusual at the moment, or the stringency of a man's finances is exceptionally severe, or the banter and ridicule of companions is peculiarly trying, or the seducing witchery of temptation is supremely potent; the man halts, hesitates, calls it a justifiable emergency, and suspends the rules. God help him! What he does he knows not now, but he shall know hereafter. At the moment, in the false perspective, he sees men as trees, walking; all things look about alike, — God like the devil, wrong like right. But afterward, oh, afterward! when the light has come, not like the broad, benignant sunrise, but like the sheeted lightning bursting in upon the night, in the glare of infamous exposure, in the blaze of shame, — afterward he shall know that the wages of sin is death.

"I see men as trees, walking." So some tend to false perspective in the spiritual life. Once, in the borders of Judæa, beyond Jordan, there came to Christ a young man of wealth, who professed to desire the spiritual life.[1] He asked that its principles might be explained to him. Christ pointed out to him that the central principle of spiritual life is the willingness to renounce self and self-chosen good, for the sake of Jesus. To the young man's eyes, full of false perspective, such a principle dealt a death-blow at the spiritual life. How could renunciation ever be more to a man than possession? How could giving up for Jesus' sake ever be chosen and loved better than having for one's own sake? He could not see it. And he went away sorrowful, for he had great possessions. Many more since his day have failed to see it. That life in the fellowship of the Son of God, where sacrifice becomes a joy, and self-renunciation for His sake the most gladdening form of self-expression; that spiritual life where the majesty and glory of things unseen is far more satisfying than physical abundance, that life is an enigma to many this day. They cannot see the charm of it. They cannot imagine wherein it becomes a successful rival with the world, for the affections and the enthusiasms of a human heart. They cannot conceive how one still hour with Jesus may be more enthralling with delight than the most

[1] St. Matt. xix. 16-26.

sumptuous pageant of the world. They cannot see it. No! nor will they, till that Touch which makes all things clear is laid on their eyes as it has been laid on some of us. Till then life will be viewed in false perspective; the things that are seen and temporal will look larger and grander and more captivating than the things that are not seen and are eternal; the trees and the men massed in the foreground will block the sky-line. Only the Touch of Jesus Christ can set it right.

Here, then, we have before us some examples of tendency to false perspective. In matters of health, of mental culture, of moral life and of spiritual life, we see the possibility of mistaken view; of that open-eyed blindness which perceives things without being able to perceive their relations. Is it necessary for me to say more than a few words concerning the evils of false perspective? We all know how many forms of physical suffering are traced by the skill of modern physicians to some defect in the eyes; till we grow almost to feel that if the eyes are right, all is right. It seems as if modern oculists, by their marvellous demonstrations of the influence of vision upon other bodily functions, are throwing new significance into Christ's words: "If thine eye be single, thy whole body shall be full of light; but if thine eye be evil, thy whole body shall be full of darkness."[1] The evils of false perspective, the sad consequences upon all the personality, following from a mistaken view of the relation of things, are as comprehensive as the maladies which relate themselves to physical disorders of the eye.

The misappropriation of energy is one of the evils of false perspective; working yourself to death for a second-rate prize. I am not speaking of man's heritage of toil; in the sweat of his brow he must earn his bread:—

> "Men must work, and women must weep,
> For there's little to earn, and many to keep;"

I am speaking of the work, the thinking, the scheming, the strength, that are thrown away on second-rate prizes. "Wherefore do ye spend money for that which is not bread; and your labor for that which satisfieth not?"[2] It is the curse of the false perspective, and the world is full of it; men selling body and soul to the devil in order to keep up a false show of wealth till they drop into that premature grave, a convict's cell; women scheming to attain that which when they have it is not worth the having; while better things, purer things, things

[1] St. Matt. vi. 22, 23.   [2] Isa. lv. 2.

great with immortality, lie mute around them unnoticed, uncomprehended, undesired.

The tyranny of non-essentials is one of the evils of false perspective. When they arrested Christ in the Garden of Gethsemane, Peter, in a fury, draws his sword, strikes into the crowd and maims Malchus, cutting off his ear.[1] "Put up your sword," says the calm Christ, with a touch as he heals the wounded ear; "To smite Malchus is false perspective. I have no quarrel with that poor man; he knows not what he does. I have a greater baptism to be baptized with; I have yet a cup to drink which is in My Father's Hand; I must get Me ready for that." Christ was too great, He saw too far, to live under the tyranny of non-essentials. He threw them off gloriously, as a ship throws off the spray on either bow. He accepted His Own real trials: He faced Gethsemane; He bent to His Cross. He went to Calvary to drink the cup of woe; but in the grand perspective of living He knew what worries He might throw aside, and with whom He need have no words. Not till His Touch is on our eyes can we see to do likewise. Till then, the tyranny of non-essentials breaks the spirit of men; petty worries, small confusions, secondary

[1] St. Matt. xxvi. 51, 52.

attacks, assume exaggerated powers; the dust of the road hides the hills to which it leads. The sudden quarrel with Malchus unnerves one for patience at the judgment bar of a bitterer trial, for majesty and peace in the supreme hour of the Cross. Who needs not to pray this prayer: "Teach me, O Master, to discern betwixt small and great in the perspective of trial, and let not a wayside brawl break up a march to Calvary!"

Let me speak, as I close this sermon, of the Touch that makes all things clear. "He laid His Hands upon him and asked him, 'Seest thou aught?' and he looked up and said, 'I see men as trees, walking.' Then again He laid His Hands upon his eyes; and he looked steadfastly and was restored, and saw all things clearly." That was the Touch that made all things clear. Has He laid it on our eyes? Has He given us through His Holy Spirit our perspective? How, then, do we look at life? Through the principles of true perspective? There are three things you will see in your perspective if His Hands have indeed been laid upon your eyes, in the Touch that makes all things clear. You will see the difference between apparent size and real size; you will see the converging lines; you will see the vanishing point.

You will see the difference between apparent size and real size. The things in the foreground are not the greatest of all; the trees and the men have apparent size, looming up close before you; but the lines that run back into the picture suggest to you now larger and larger things; the spaces of life, the scale of the mountains, the shore of the sea.

You will see the converging lines. As the lines move on in the picture, they draw together. Is this, then, the perspective of living, to realize that the lines of things are not parallel, running on endlessly side by side? They are converging lines, drawing closer and closer together as they move.

You will see the vanishing point. It is not in the picture to be seen, but your mind tells you it is there; a point where all the long converging lines meet at last to vanish in infinity. On and on, then, must be our thought of living; on and on, beneath the Touch that makes all things clear. We cannot be stopped in the confusion of the foreground; on and on, in thought, in prayer, in hope, in service, till the long lines meet where sea and sky are one — and vanish in eternity! Amen.

IX.

THE BENEDICTION OF THE RISEN LORD.

IX.

THE BENEDICTION OF THE RISEN LORD.

Preached on Easter Day, 1889.

"Then came Jesus and stood in the midst, and saith unto them, Peace be unto you. Then said Jesus to them again, Peace be unto you. And after eight days again came Jesus, and stood in the midst and said, Peace be unto you." — St. John xx. 19, 21, 26.

WE are to speak of the Benediction of the Risen Lord. Sometimes in summer, after a three days' storm, there dawns a morning when the air is clear as crystal, soft as a child's breath, still as heaven. The pitiless east wind that tore the trees, that screamed like the nighthawk, that lashed the sea into tawny foam; the sheets of rain that travelled on the roaring blast, that swelled the streams, that beat at the windows; the low-hanging clouds, over whose leaden fronts have swept the interminable fringes of flying scud, — all these have vanished at midnight, and with the dawn have come beauty, and calmness, and untroubled glory. The sea is still, giving back the blue of a cloudless sky; the air sparkles with light thrown out from the rain-baptism on trees and lawns; and overhead, as through a "sapphire sea," the sun "sails like a golden galleon." This magnificent contrast in nature is no unworthy type of that majestic and consoling tranquillity with which the Resurrection morning dawns out of the awful strife, the unimaginable sorrow, the enormous gloom, surrounding the Cross and Grave of Jesus Christ.

Reflect for a moment upon the concentrated violence of pain, confusion, ignominy, horror and destruction which charged the hours from Gethsemane to the Entombment. Remember the Agony and Bloody Sweat; remember the hideous betrayal by an apostle; remember the ignominy of those investigations pursued before the ecclesiastical and the civil tribunals. Remember the mockery and the castigation; remember the roar of that cry of hatred, "Crucify Him! Crucify Him!" remember the deathly march to Calvary; remember the shock and tension when the cross was uplifted; remember the ferocious confusion that raged about Him as He was slowly dying; remember the darkness and the earthquake; remember the Voice that issued from that ghastly gloom, carrying up to God a message God only could interpret: "My God, My God, why hast Thou forsaken Me?" Then, turning from that "horrible tempest" of strife and sorrow and gloom, look upon the morning of beauty and calmness amidst which Jesus enters on His Resurrection Life. From the moment of His Resurrection, strife, pain, pressure, agony, confusion have no power over Him. Silently as the morning climbs the summer sky, He moves from place to place; gentle and radiant as sunlight is His Presence, Who lately was bowed by the travail of His Soul; and when He speaks, His first words to the believing circle strike the keynote of all He would do for us, and be in us, and bring to us evermore; the Benediction of the Risen Lord: "Peace be unto you."

Three times within the octave of Easter Day did He pronounce that Benediction, as though He would make clear at the very outset, to the believing Church, that the Risen Lord longs to bring and to keep peace in these hearts of ours, however fierce the strife, however long the warfare, through which we must go. "The first day of the week came Jesus, and stood in the midst and saith unto them, Peace be unto you. Then said Jesus to them again, Peace be unto you; and after eight days again came Jesus, and stood in the midst and said unto them, Peace be unto you."

Each time He uttered that Benediction, He threw into it a new meaning by combining with it some gracious act or word. The first time we read, "Jesus stood in the midst and said unto them, Peace be unto you. And when He had so said, He shewed unto them His Hands and His Side." Thus He connects His Benediction of peace with His Own sufferings, reminding us that the chastisement of our peace is upon Him, and by His stripes we are healed. Peace, true peace, is for those to whom the meaning of the sufferings of Jesus is disclosed; for those to whom He has shown His Hands and His Side.

The second time we read: "Then said Jesus to them again, Peace be unto you: as My Father hath sent Me, even so send I you. And when He had said this, He breathed on them and said, Receive ye the Holy Ghost." Thus He connects His Benediction of peace with His gift of the Holy Spirit, Who alone can make peace and keep peace in our hearts amid the disquietudes, disappointments, and bereavements of this life. He not only bids us be at peace, but He imparts to us that Holy Comforter Who is the Author of peace. "He breathed on them and said, Receive ye the Holy Ghost."

The third time we read: "After eight days again came Jesus, and stood in the midst and said, Peace be unto you. Then said He to Thomas, Reach hither thy finger and behold My Hands, and reach hither thy hand and thrust it into My Side, and be not faithless but believing." Thus He connects His Benediction of peace with an appeal to our faith. He invites us, in our trouble, in our anxiety, and in our tension, to draw very near to Him, to lay our hand in His wounded Hand; to surrender our minds to Him with the trustful simplicity of little children; to find peace in believing. Thus, attended by the reference to His Own sufferings, by the offer of His Holy Spirit, and by the affectionate appeal to our faith, the first words of the Risen Saviour to His believing Church come to us.

The first words of our risen friends! How eagerly we shall listen to them when, for each one of us in turn who have watched by the bedsides of our beloved, "earth breaks up and heaven expands;" and we, treading the gateway of Paradise, are met and welcomed by those who have gone before us! With what passionate eagerness of attention we strain our ears to catch the last broken, failing utterances of the dying; how our very senses seem sharpened into sevenfold keenness as we bend over those stricken lips whispering their farewells; and when the murmuring grows inarticulate, and the speaking eyes can alone utter the love message, how breathlessly we wait for one more possible word which never comes! And as the years go by, how we repeat to ourselves the last dear, imperishable words; how we summon our faithful memory to recall the last glowing look of affection! But if we thus prize the last words of dying friends, shall we not be yet more glad to hear the first words of risen friends when we meet them again in Paradise? Think of the experiences they are having, while we have lived on without them; think of the companionship they are having with the true-hearted and the holy on high; think of the splendors they are seeing, before the throne of God and of the Lamb; think of the thoughts they are thinking about us! What will their first words of greeting be? Which of all their bright experiences will they want us first to share?

Let us remember that all the wonderful significance and affection and heavenly joy, which we involuntarily associate with the first words of our risen friends, we may associate with the Benedictions of the Risen Lord. They are to us believers the first words of our Risen Friend. They are the words with which He breaks the silence of the grave. "Peace be unto you! Peace be unto you! Peace be unto you!" A threefold prayer for our peace.

It is good for us, my brethren, whose lot it is to dwell in this exciting and fatiguing age, to remember on this Easter morning that the first words of our Risen Friend are a Benediction of peace. For I fear that you as well as I, who are in the thick of the fight, who feel the startling rapidity of changes, who are subject to that high tension of mind and spirit characteristic of these times, — I fear that you and I are tempted sometimes to ask, Is there any peace? Does that white dove still brood over any heart, or is the whole world given over to anxiety, and toil, and pressure, and fear? It may be that I am only growing older, and seeing in my turn what others have seen before me; but certainly I am profoundly and continually conscious of the prevailing anxiety, and strain, and multiplication of cares, in the lives of those about me, and often I am at a loss to find evidence that Christians are tasting any holy calm and repose of spirit above that which is known by others. There are undoubtedly forces active in modern life which tend to destroy our first impressions of the possibility of peace. It is beyond question that men are generally working with more rapidity now than formerly. The machinery of life is accelerated. The intelligence of the age is concentrated on this problem, — the maximum of results in the minimum of time. It is beyond question, too, that interests have multiplied, quite as rapidly as the rate of working. The rapid working has not increased the seasons of leisure, because the bulk of work to do has grown with the rate of doing. Such intensity has its own brilliant rewards, but, no less, its own heavy costs. Pressure has now become a second nature to most men, and habitual pressure, unless there be some Divine counteraction, becomes the great antagonist of peace.

Yet never was it more true than on this blessed Easter Day that the great Benediction of our Risen Lord is peace. This is His first, His great desire for us. He stands in our midst and says, "Peace be unto you." He to Whom our hearts are open, our desires known, and from Whom none of our secrets are hid, stands in our midst on this great day of commemoration, looking with the searching Eyes of Love into the depths of each life. He knows our pressure; the strain on nerve and brain for those who are fighting the battle of existence, — toiling, for their own sake and for the love of dear ones, through opposition and through calamity. He knows our care: the burden of the interests of others; the training, guiding, helping work that must be done and done again; the responsibility of station and office, of parental headship, of social accountability. He knows our spiritual struggle: the importunity of unsanctified impulses, the humiliating sting of moral failure; the exhausting aspirations after the Divine knowledge. He knows our human sorrow: the pang of sudden grief; the slow heartache of accomplished bereavement; the restless hunger of wounded affections; the burial of reasonable and holy hopes. All these the Risen Saviour knows: yet, as He stands in our midst, His first words are, "Peace be unto you." Christ Who died for us would not mock us. He would not say to us, "Peace, peace, when there is no peace."[1] The Benediction of the Risen Lord must point to a peace which for the Christian is attainable and maintainable amidst the actual conditions which make up life.

If this be so, we know then that the peace which Christ wishes for us in His Easter Benediction is not the peace which comes from the

[1] Jer. vi. 14.

absence of care. How impracticable would such a wish be! Who can live at all, and live without care, unless it be the most selfish and gross of lives? Who can have any breadth of purpose, any generosity of effort, any depth of feeling, without taking on care? Who that has the spirit of a true man, or the spirit of a true woman, would ask, even if the request could be granted, a life without care? Every relationship that ennobles life brings care with it; and the more holy and vital that relationship the more care is risked in our assumption of it. And we may also be sure that the peace which Christ wishes for us in His Easter Benediction is not the peace which comes from the absence of sorrow. For who can escape sorrow unless the heart has first been turned to marble? Why should God have placed within you that measureless possibility of suffering if you are not made to suffer? The absence of sorrow! Think what it would mean! It would mean that you could see your neighbor's home desolated, his wife and his child swept from his side, without one momentary interruption of your own pleasure. It would mean that you could see the imploring eyes of your own dying child turned upon you without one pang shooting through your being. It would mean that you could see your Saviour perish on the cross for your sake without one outburst of contrition from your stony consciousness. The absence of sorrow? God forbid! Christ could not wish us to have peace like that; brute-peace. Nay, my brethren! the glory of Christ's Easter Benediction is, that it contemplates a life such as our life is, with the possibilities of care, pressure, bereavement, and pain by which we are continually surrounded; it tells us of a peace which one may have in his life when the storms of care are raging around him, when the goads of pressure are driven into him; it tells of a peace which may flow like a river through the deeper depths of consciousness when the anguish of bereavement is tearing the affections, and when the paroxysms of pain are torturing the body.

What is that peace? Let us look back to the Resurrection Day, and read the deeper meanings of the Saviour's Benediction, as with each utterance of the words, "Peace be unto you," He makes some sign, or speaks some word, disclosing His meaning.

"Peace be unto you! and when He had so said, He showed them His Hands and His Side." Our Risen Saviour would have us find our peace in remembering His sufferings. In this assembly, outwardly serene and attentive, there may be many persons sorely tried in mind, body, or estate. Our own griefs, or the griefs of our friends, may weigh upon us so heavily that human nature cries out impulsively, " Is it right, can it be right, that there should be such suffering?" To us the Saviour answers by showing us His Hands and His Side. These are the outward symbols of an inward suffering such as man has never known. These are the outward symbols of an inward suffering so immeasurably beyond all that man has suffered, that He Who has endured such suffering can stand in the fellowship of all who suffer, and can yet say, "I have trodden the wine-press alone."[1] We ask, Why did He suffer? "Christ also hath once suffered for sins that He might bring us to God."[2] And now day by day, as this mysterious necessity of suffering is asserting itself in our lives, as in turn one after another of these households and of these souls passes through its Gethsemane, the Risen Lord comes daily, hourly, to His people saying, " Peace be unto you. Think not that suffering means separation from the love of God. Behold My Hands and My Side."

" And He said unto them again: Peace be

[1] Isa. lxiii. 3.   [2] 1 Pet. iii. 18.

unto you; and when He had said this, He breathed on them and said, Receive ye the Holy Ghost." Our Risen Saviour would have us find our peace through the grace of the Holy Comforter. That the Christian may be calm in the midst of cares and worries, patient under pain, submissive under sorrow, he has more power at his command than comes from a strong will, or from a naturally patient disposition. And where the will is not naturally strong, and the disposition is not naturally patient, it is not right for us to say that we are at a hopeless disadvantage. For the Risen Lord, Who speaks the Benediction of peace, sends the Author and Agent of peace into our hearts, breathing upon us and saying, "Receive ye the Holy Ghost." And to-day, in this age of haste and pressure and vicissitude, that Holy Peacemaker is working in many lives; and I know that in this Easter service there are many who feel that their powers of courage, and calmness, and conquering trust this day are not the product of strong human wills and patient human dispositions, but are the product of the Grace of the Comforter Whom they have received, breathed upon them by the Risen Lord, and dwelling now within them; creating an inward sanctuary of holy peace and heavenly harmony as they move through a stormy and difficult world.

> "There are in this loud stunning tide
> Of human care and crime,
> With whom the melodies abide
> Of th' everlasting chime;
> Who carry music in their heart
> Through dusky lane and wrangling mart,
> Plying their task with busier feet
> Because their secret souls a holy strain repeat."[1]

" And after eight days again came Jesus, and stood in the midst and said unto them, Peace be unto you. Then saith He to Thomas, Reach hither thy finger, and behold My Hands, and reach hither thy hand and thrust it into My Side, and be not faithless but believing." Our Risen Saviour in His Easter Benediction appeals to our faith. He asks us to believe Him; to lay hold of Him with trustful hands; to acknowledge Him as our Lord and our God; to let Him lead us where He will. It is the secret of peace, which the world knoweth not because it knows Him not. No philosophy can explain away the mysteries of this human life. None can adjust its contradictions, nor remove its distresses. The mysteries, contradictions, distresses, still are there, after all is said and done, but God gives us the choice between the fretful

---

[1] Keble: *St. Matthew's Day.*

protest of our unsatisfied reason and the calm confession of our faith in the Risen Lord; and in the hour when the troubled and terrified heart of man yields a childlike trust to God, in the hour when the helpless hand of human wisdom is placed in the wounded Hands of Jesus Christ, the Benediction of Him Who lives to die no more is accomplished in us, and the distress of doubting passes into the peace of believing.

> "Peace, perfect peace, in this dark world of sin?
> The Blood of Jesus whispers peace within.
>
> "Peace, perfect peace, by thronging duties pressed?
> To do the will of Jesus, this is rest.
>
> "Peace, perfect peace, with loved ones far away?
> In Jesus' keeping, we are safe, and they.
>
> "Peace, perfect peace, our future all unknown?
> Jesus we know, and He is on the Throne."[1]

[1] E. H. Bickersteth, Bishop of Exeter.

X.
THE UNFORGOTTEN LABOURERS.

X.

THE UNFORGOTTEN LABOURERS.

PREACHED ON NOVEMBER 2, 1890.

"Other men laboured, and ye are entered into their labours."—ST. JOHN iv. 38.

IT is with a heart full of gratitude to those who have lived, and toiled, and aspired, and suffered, and died before us, that I speak of The Unforgotten Labourers. "Other men laboured, and ye are entered into their labours." I trust I may never lose, beneath the multiplicity of later impressions, the impression that was made upon me of our indebtedness to those who have gone before us, and of the charge we have received from their hands, when, sixteen years ago yesterday, I beheld Charles Kingsley arise in Westminster Abbey, and preach the All-Saints'-Day Sermon. The light of that eternity, upon which within three months he was destined to enter, appeared even then to rest upon his face, as he spoke of those who came out of the great tribulation, who have washed their robes and made them white in the Blood of the Lamb, and who are before the Throne of God. Well has it been said of that sermon by her who knew him best: "It will never be forgotten by those who heard it. It was like a note of preparation for the life of eternal blessedness in the vision of God, upon which he himself was so soon to enter."[1]

I am not sorry to find that, as life has moved onward from that day, reverence for the workers of the past, and delight in commemorating the Unforgotten Labourers, have appeared to deepen with the years; and that there come times when these emotions command expression. I do not see that it makes one any less broad, any less eager in his work, — certainly it does not make one any less humble and careful, — to realize how much of all we do is simply entering into conditions and possibilities created for us by the Unforgotten Labourers.

The principle enunciated by our Saviour, as He presses home upon His disciples a sense of their responsibility, saying, "I sent you to reap that on which ye bestowed no labour; other men laboured, and ye are entered into their labours," is one of the principles most con-

---

[1] *Charles Kingsley: His Letters and Memories of his Life*, edited by his Wife, vol. ii. p. 450. Tenth ed.

stantly and most seriously illustrated, nobly and ignobly, in the history of human affairs of all kinds, — national, social, and personal. It is easy to name at once four ways, in secular affairs, in which men may be said to have entered into the labours of other men. They have entered by Invasion, or by Indolence, or by Industry, or by Inheritance. When the army of occupation enters a foreign territory, reduces its defences, besieges its capital, unseats its government, and claims its revenues, it enters by Invasion into the labours of other men. When the nerveless, inglorious sluggard relies on others to do the work he should be doing, allows himself to be supported after the day when he should aspire to be the support of some dependent life, he enters by Indolence into the labours of others. When the indomitable student masters a great poem, explores a great treatise, applies a great discovery, he enters by Industry into the labours of others. When the child, grown man, putting away childish things, takes with his manhood the legacy of an honored father's name, and assumes the high position constituted by his father's faithfulness, he enters by Inheritance into the labours of another. Thus, in ways both weak and strong, in ways inglorious, in ways noble and worthy, this principle finds manifold application on the field of ordinary human affairs.

But when the soul, whom Christ has ordained to serve Him, lifts up its eyes to the Master's Face to learn how wide is service, and how high is service, and how long is service, Christ has His wonderful way of interpreting to us the width, and height, and length of service. What is His way? Listen to one of the "stories of old." Long ago the heart of a young man was full of fear when he beheld the thronging enemies that gathered around him and around his prophet-master.[1] And he cried, "Alas, my master! how shall we do?" And the prophet-master answered: "Fear not, for they that be with us are more than they that be with them." And the prophet-master prayed and said: "Lord, I pray thee, open his eyes that he may see." And the Lord opened the eyes of the young man and he saw, and, behold, the mountain was full of horses and chariots of fire. Even thus there comes to Christ, the Greater Prophet-Master, the soul charged with the longing to make life somewhat grander than a service of self, the longing to climb that Godward path of the moun-

[1] 2 Kings vi. 15-23.

tain, that rises upward, ever upward, above things base and mean, unto things unselfish, ungrudging, undefiled. And, coming to the Prophet-Master, he asks, "What shall I do? How shall I do?" And the Prophet-Master opens his eyes to see that Godward path he seeks to climb, and, lo! it is thronged, up to the very top, down to the very bottom where he stands. A multitude whom no man can number he sees with his opened eyes. They are full of unlikeness, yet full of likeness, — full of unlikeness in their earthly beginnings, for they are of all nations and kindreds and peoples and tongues; full of unlikeness in their natural advantage, for some are crowned as with coronets, and some are in coarse raiment; full of unlikeness in their natural strength, for some are men and some are women, and many are children; some are strong and some are suffering. Yet full of likeness! for the same Light is on their faces as they climb, and the same glad love is in their hearts. And the soul that has come to the Prophet-Master asks: "What are these, and whence came they?" And the Prophet-Master answers, "These are the Unforgotten Labourers. See them. Remember them. Enter into their labours."

To-day the Prophet-Master stands among us,

and opens our eyes to see that far-reaching company of the Unforgotten Labourers who have gone on before us, setting their feet where we would set our own; preparing the way, that we may not miss it; doing so much we need not do again; opening so much for us to do, which, but for them, we could not have done, — we might not even have desired to do; showing us what can be done, that we may have faith to try also to do it. And as the Prophet-Master opens our eyes, we see that many of those faces are faces we have known, — faces that we have seen flushed with energy, or pallid with fatigue, or wet with tears, or furrowed with suffering, that they might keep in that path of service for our sake who would come after them. And the Prophet-Master simply says, " Other men laboured, and ye are entered into their labours!"

" Other men laboured!" This is our Spiritual Ancestry! Pause a moment, earnest heart, while before us remains this vision of the Godward path, thronged with the Unforgotten Labourers, and think of that continuity of spiritual life which runs in our veins, and runs back from us, through all the Unforgotten Labourers, straight to Him Who first, by the Might of His Own Example, and then by the Mystery of

His Cross and Passion, taught men to desire to die unto sin and live unto righteousness; to desire to spend and be spent for the sake of others. This is the unwritten Book of the Genealogy of Jesus Christ. In the Gospel of St. Matthew we read that human pedigree of Christ, traced step by step from David down to Him Who is both David's Son and David's Lord. But through the unbroken succession of the Unforgotten Labourers, we, if the Spirit of Christ is ours, can trace our spiritual lineage back through those who have gone before us, heart before heart, heart before heart, till we reach the Heart that came not to be ministered unto but to minister, and to give Its Life a ransom for many. Who is not stronger for remembering, amidst that appalling loneliness which at times overtakes every one who essays to live above self and above the world, — who is not stronger for remembering that we ourselves are links in that bright chain, the genealogy of kindred spirits knit together, the known and the unknown, in one communion, reaching back over the wastes of nineteen centuries; grappled at last, as with hooks of steel, to the very Manhood of the Son of God!

Other men laboured! This is the Brotherhood of Experience! Who has not felt, at times overpoweringly, the individuality of his own mission, shuddering with dread before the unexplored newness of life! The conditions of his existence seem combined according to a new formula, whereof none has ever held the key or seen the resultant. It is so awful to live and to know so little of the meaning of life; to realize that what we are set to do or to undo, to carry or to put away, to conquer or to crucify, is so unlike that which is given to others; to feel that we have been flung upon this dangerous shore of life as empty-handed and as ignorant as the shipwrecked sailor swept upon a land of which he knows not so much as the name! —

> "Alone to land upon that shore
> With no one sight that we have seen before, —
>   Things of a different hue
>   And sounds all strange and new, —
> No forms of earth for fancy to arrange,
> But to begin alone that mighty change."[1]

And then the Prophet-Master simply says to us, "Other men laboured!" and in that word we remember the Brotherhood of Experience: we know that we are not the first to be flung upon life's dangerous coast with no man to tell the way; not the first to encounter the peril of choice, the grim finality of decision;

[1] F. W. Faber, D. D.

not the first to feel the currents of adversity dragging backward around us like the undertow; not the first to call and hear no answer come out of that chill, impenetrable fogbank of the Yet To Be! Other men laboured! Ah, yes! Why should we shrink back from that which has been accepted so cheerfully, endured so splendidly, many, many times? Why should we feel that we were singled out for a new vocation of pain, or privation, or doubt, or loneliness, or care, or toil, and not acknowledge that in all these things we are but brethren to the Unforgotten Labourers? Why should we complain, as though an unjust pressure were put upon us; or fret, as if the pain were cruelty; or debate, as though perchance love had leaked away out of God's Heart, — when we know that other men laboured? We may be swept on some desolate shore, but there before us is the footprint of a man. We may be shut up in a very narrow prison, but there, cut in the stone, is the signature of a saint. Other men laboured: —

> "Where now with pain thou treadest, trod
> The whitest of the Saints of God!
> To show thee where their feet were set,
> The light which led them shineth yet." [1]

And ye are entered into their labours! As

[1] John Greenleaf Whittier.

we pass to this part of this great Word of the Prophet-Master, a new light seems to fall on that long file of the Unforgotten Labourers toiling up before us on the mountain of God; and not only to fall on them but to fall on us, showing us how truly and how grandly we are with them and of them; that they could not complete their purposes without us, and we could not attain our victory without them. "Ye," says Christ, "are entered into their labours." We have entered in as their heirs, — they have transmitted an inheritance. They had set their love upon us, seeing us afar off, and desiring to make the way of truth more clear and glorious in our eyes. Not for themselves did they live above themselves and above the world; not for themselves have the Unforgotten Labourers laid on the Altar of Sacrifice strength, wealth, labor, safety, — yes, even life itself; not for themselves have they endured the Cross, despising the shame; not for themselves have they left us an example that we should follow their steps, in the pureness of their mind, in the patience of their gentleness, in the courage of their faith, in the fidelity of their love, in the zeal of their work. "They dreamt not of a perishable home who thus could build." No! Those who have had within them most richly of the Spirit of Christ have most intensely lived for those who were coming after them, esteeming themselves to have succeeded best if they might hand on to us undefiled the Ark of Truth, and mark for others, though it were with their own blood, the path that leads at last to the Light. Ah, blessed ones! pure ones! who have loved us and have aspired for us; who, in their own sorrows, have anticipated ours, and have tried to leave on record that which might be to us a sign to conquer by; who in their own aspirations have tried to lift us, "as the eagle fluttereth over her young, spreadeth abroad her wings, taketh them, beareth them on her wings,"[1] — they have transmitted an inheritance unto us, those Unforgotten Labourers, and we are entered into their labours! "How large a part of our Godward life is travelled, not by clear landmarks seen far off in the promised land, but as travellers climb a mountain peak, by putting footstep after footstep, slowly and patiently, into the prints which some one, going before us, with keener sight, with stronger nerves, tied to us by the chord of saintly sympathy, has planted deep into the pathless snow of the bleak distance that

[1] Deut. xxxii. 11.

stretches up between humanity and God! We ascend by one another. No man liveth to himself, and no man dieth to himself. We live and die, not only to God, but to each other."[1]

"Other men laboured, and ye are entered into their labours!" If upon any of us has fallen with power this thought of the Unforgotten Labourers; if we have been led to think to-day of the love a father or a mother, a brother, a sister, or a friend, bore toward us; of the efforts after completeness they made for our sake; of the inheritance of opportunity they transmitted unto us; and if, thinking out upon wider lines, we have gathered in remembrance all who loved us, who trusted in us, and who have gone before us up that wondrous mountain-path, — how shall this thought come in and temper our characters from this day forward? Shall it not make us truly humble and truly brave?

Truly humble, I say. Not falsely and untruly humble, with vain and insincere attempts at self-depreciation, speaking of our God-given powers as poor and mean. Not this, but truly humble, as we remember how much of our best labour is and must continue to be but an entering into the labours of others; how much of our finest life is altogether conditioned on the

[1] Bishop Phillips Brooks.

genius, or the fidelity, or the sacrifice, or the suffering of those who have gone before us; how much of our most advanced and aggressive work is possible only because Unforgotten Labourers have laid, in courses of tears, the twelvefold foundations on which we build our heavenliest superstructures. Yes! truly humble, as we remember "the saints who from their labours rest;" the merciful, the poor in spirit, the meek, the pure in heart, the peacemakers, the persecuted for righteousness' sake. How easy to find among them a Better to crown our best, a Greater to include and soar above our greatest!

And shall it not make us truly brave, — oh, for once and forever truly brave; not falsely and vainly brave, in the emptiness of boasting, in the cheap disparagement of the awfulness of living; but truly brave through the sense of kinship with Unforgotten Labourers " who through faith subdued kingdoms, wrought righteousness, obtained promises, stopped the mouths of lions, quenched the violence of fire, out of weakness were made strong, waxed valiant in fight, turned to flight the armies of the aliens"?[1] Yes, truly brave, when we remember that we are kin to those of whom the world

[1] Heb. xi. 33, 34.

was not worthy; who had greater pressure than we, yet were not broken under it; greater disappointment than we, yet were not embittered by it; greater temptation than we, yet were not vanquished before it; greater mystery than we, yet were not hopeless amidst it. These all died in faith, making, every one of them, life seem to some one else forever a nobler, wider, worthier thing; helping, every one of them, goodness and purity and patience and the conquest of self to demonstrate themselves to some one else as the very evidences of Christ; leaving, every one of them, sunk deep in the heart of some one else an unconquerable passion to be strong as they were strong. And we are kin to them, those Unforgotten Labourers; next in line to some of them we stand, amongst those who have essayed in Christ to climb that mountain path, and to rise above self! Can we drop out where they went on? — we fear to watch with Him one bitter or one arduous hour, when they kept vigil till the day broke? It must not be. It cannot be. Please God, it shall not be, if the spirit of our life be the spirit of that supplication poured from a human heart hundreds of years ago (the prayer of Thomas Aquinas), "Give me, O Jesus, a wakeful heart, which no curious imagination may withdraw from Thee; give me a steadfast heart, which no unworthy affection may drag downward; give me an unconquered heart, which no tribulation can wear out; give me a free and disengagèd heart, which the violence of no absorbing fascination may enslave; give me an upright heart, which no unworthy purpose may tempt aside." Amen.

XI.

THE GIFT OF ADVERSITY.

XI.

THE GIFT OF ADVERSITY.

"Though the Lord give you the bread of adversity and the water of affliction, thine eyes shall see thy teachers; and thine ears shall hear a word behind thee saying, This is the way; walk ye in it." — ISAIAH xxx. 20, 21.

WE have approached a subject which can only be touched, if touched at all in open speech, with the greatest reverence, with the greatest tenderness, and with the greatest delicacy, — The Gift of Adversity. There are three reasons which can immediately be given why it is difficult to speak upon this theme. One reason is, one knows so little of the extent of adversity in the lives around him. It is of the nature of prosperity to reveal itself; like the vigorous plant, it tends boldly out into the joyous sunlight, and unfolds its beauty to the eyes of others. It is of the nature of adversity to hide itself within a sensitive life. Instinctively we draw the robe of a dignified concealment over our wounded spirit, and prefer to suffer unobserved. Therefore one who ventures to speak of adversity feels, almost with awe, how little he knows where his words may fall on pained and overburdened hearts. Another reason is: One fears lest his words may sound superficial to those who are in the school of adversity; that some may say to him in their hearts, "Ah, you do not know. If you knew you would not say it," forgetting, perhaps, that God has many ways of giving us knowledge of the gift of adversity. And yet another reason is, that sometimes the heart resents the effort to reconcile it to adversity. It refuses to be comforted. Its adversity is so bitter and so unwelcome the heart is alienated from its lot, repudiates its cross, loathes its meagre fare of bread and water, struggling restively to shake off its chain. For these reasons, it is no light matter to speak of adversity.

But, on the other hand, it is a most blessed subject on which to speak. One is so certain, in speaking, to find fellowship in many other lives, who, like one's self, have caught, however dimly, the thought that adversity must, in some way, be a gift of God; that it cannot all be a mistake, a lapse and breakdown of His plan, much less a visitation of His anger; that it must be in the plan, and in the love, and unto the "best" that "is yet to be." One is so certain, in speaking, that others all around him have had Christ made known unto them in the breaking of the bread of adversity, in the pouring out of the water of affliction, — have had the Real Presence in the holy sacrament of hardship, have heard through pain and fear the whisper of that dear Guardian Who follows ever behind us, saying, " This is the way ; walk ye in it."

What is adversity? Adversity is not merely the loss of money. The loss of money may, and continually does, create a state of adversity, but it is one of the incidental causes of that state, which may also be brought about by an infinite number of other causes as well; insomuch that there may be the most bitter adversity in a life whose money matters are all in good condition. The clue to the real nature of adversity is found in the word itself, " Adversus," that which is against us, contrary to us, in opposition to our hopes, our desires, our expectations, or our efforts. The failure of bodily strength, so that the ambitious and willing spirit can no more control the fainting and suffering flesh, but must go halting or maimed, or internally tortured, — this is adversity. The embarrassment of our fortunes, so that hopes once considered reasonable are wrecked by the weakness of another, and life is made one desperate, heart-sickening chase to overtake our pecuniary obligations, — this is adversity. The postponement of plans, with life slipping by, and the ardent heart aching to express itself in greater ways; yet stolid obstacles standing in the path, and bolted doors of necessity shutting in the eager mind, — this is adversity. The withheld completion of desire, when the skilled and gentle hands remain empty-handed, when the hungering outgoings of affection remain unappeased; when "the thing prayed for comes" hopelessly "short of the prayer," — this is adversity. The shattering of an ideal, so that love and trust are profaned, joyous certitude transmuted into gnawing doubt, hero-worship beaten to the ground, and belief in goodness savagely shaken, — this is adversity. The shadow of death! falling at noonday on our beloved; quenching the beams of mental clearness, hushing the silvery voice of greeting, spreading through the once joyous home the gloom of fearful sickness, the lamentations of bereavement, — this is adversity.

Yes, these are adversity, and others like unto them, every one like all the rest in this: it is in our life the expression of the "Adversus," of that which is against us, and opposed to us, from the standpoint of our hopes, desires, expectations, or efforts. And who amongst us all has not known in some degree, small or great, the sensation of being met by the "Adversus," standing like a veiled angel in our path, blocking the way, and, when from our impetuous heart breaks the "I will," "I must," calmly answering, "And thou shalt not." O mysterious figure! veiled angel of the "Adversus!" whence art thou? Art thou the enemy of God rising from the dark depths beneath to thwart Him, to confuse His plans, to block His way, to keep us from entering into the completeness He has it in His Heart to give us? or art thou the messenger and gift of God, sent down from the Father of Lights, from Whom cometh every good and perfect gift, to bless us by opposing us, to enrich us by impoverishing us, to turn us back from going our way that we may find a more excellent way, that we may be guided into all truth? Whence is adversity? Is it all a mistake and a catastrophe, and an evidence of failure, that in this world so much is as we would not have it be, so much is not as we prayed it might be? Is it all wrong, and confusion, and the losing of the way, that, for so many, life is other than they hope, other than they desire, other than they endeavor to make it? Or can this be, not a break in the plan, but a part of the plan? Can this be, not a gloomy catastrophe, but an order, a spiritual order; not a discord, but an involved harmony, to be resolved, through marvellous intervals, into the clear " C major " of a perfected life? Can it be?

Listen! The one thing that I seek most carefully not to do is to idealize adversity, to tell you that pain is not pain, that sorrow is not sorrow, that heart-hunger and unrest are not the devastating things they seem to be. How could one even wish — much more, how could one dare — to call pain by any other name than pain, or sorrow by any other name than sorrow, when the Holy Ghost hath said " no chastening for the present seemeth to be joyous, but grievous?"[1] But if the one thing that I seek most carefully not to do is to commit the vanity of idealizing adversity, and of preaching any painless pain, the one thing that I most desire to do is to speak of what new powers and certainties may come into a life and be forevermore a part of it, what new seeings and what new hearings, if a soul can in any way be brought to look upon adversity as a gift from the Father, — a sacrament of bread and water administered by the very Hand of God; a true

[1] Heb. xii. 11.

communion ordinance. Can I speak to you of this? Will you have patience with me while I speak of the new seeing and the new hearing which come to those who bend in communion at this Life-Altar of Sacrifice, and who take out of God's Hand the Holy Elements, the bread of adversity and the water of affliction? "Though the Lord give you the bread of adversity and the water of affliction, thine eyes shall see thy teachers, and thine ears shall hear a word behind thee saying, This is the way; walk ye in it."

You will perhaps have observed, before I point out the thought to you, that three elementary factors of our life stand related in this verse, — eating, seeing, hearing. God is represented as giving one a portion of food, and, lo! for him who eats it the eyes are opened to see one's teachers, and the ears are quickened to hear that gentle word of reassurance nerving one with courage to go on: "This is the way, walk thou in it."

There could hardly be a more profound way of setting before our minds what it is to accept adversity, than as it is here represented under the elements of bread and water, given and received: "Though the Lord give you the bread of adversity and the water of affliction."

It is wonderful to group together the apparently incongruous ideas which are presented to our minds in the associations connected with bread and water. Bread and water are prison fare, the most meagre and joyless table in the world, spread for him who is deprived of liberty and of light, who is appointed for the discipline of loneliness, of suffering, and perchance of death. But bread and water are also the great universal supports of life; they are the primal elements of man's strength in all countries, in all grades of society, in all periods of the world. Men of unrelated races may not understand each other's ways of living, may look with amazement upon the foods which in various countries are considered articles of luxury; but where could two men of opposite nationalities be found who would not understand and hold in common the elements of bread and water? Bread and water are both of them taken by Christ as types of Himself, in what He is, in what He can bestow: "I am the bread of life;"[1] "Whosoever drinketh of the water that I shall give him shall never thirst."[2] They become, therefore, associated with all that is most rich in itself, with all that is most spiritually satisfying to those who can

[1] St. Jno. vi. 48.   [2] St. Jno. iv. 14.

receive it; they are the emblems of Him in Whom it was the good pleasure of the Father that all the fulness should dwell.[1] And now we are asked to think of them as sacramental emblems of that many-sided adversity which, in one form or another, is so certainly to be presented to us for our acceptance. And with all these different thoughts of bread and water standing together in our minds, — bread and water as the wretched, joyless prison fare; bread and water as the elements of food which all men share in common; bread and water as types of the gracious fulness of Christ, — let us think of them as sacramental emblems of adversity offered to us in the Hand of God, the bread of adversity and the water of affliction.

You look at them and you say: "Prison fare, meagre and wretched; take them away. I want better food." Dear friend, I cannot blame you if you say that, for pain is pain, and sorrow is sorrow, and disappointment is disappointment, and they are all prison fare, meagre and joyless and repulsive. Who wants to live like that? Who does not turn away sickened from the diet of adversity to think of the bright and bounteous feasts of prosperity?

Bread and water! Look again, and you see

[1] Col. i. 18.

that they are elements, — elements of all human life, everywhere, always. Who in health has ever lived altogether without them? Who in health could live altogether without them? What, then, has been a part of human life, always, everywhere, and for all, cannot be an accident, or an exception under some larger rule, or an unmitigated evil. It must be a part of the thing itself that we call life. Would it be well for any one of us to be exempted from that which has been offered always and everywhere and unto all? Would it be reasonable to believe that for you alone, of all humanity, greater completeness could be had outside of the rule than inside of the rule? Must not this mystical bread and water of adversity and affliction be in some way necessary to man, since they are as universal as life, — as universal as death?

Bread and water! Look again! These things are chosen emblems of Christ as well as emblems of adversity. He is bread and He is water in the fulness and the richness of His capacity to feed the hunger of man's soul and to quench his thirst. And we know that He ate of the bread of adversity and drank of the water of affliction; He condescended to live on the prison fare, and to take into Himself the primal elements of human experience. And therein we all feel that He lost not of His fulness but gained; and "in that He Himself hath suffered being tempted, He is able also to succour them that are tempted."[1] What then: can it be that if we, like Him, accept these things as from the Father, and so eat of this bread and drink of this water, we, like Him, shall gain, and not lose, the fulness of our character? "Take, eat," He says, as He lays in our hand the bread of adversity. "Drink ye all of it," He says, and offers us the water of affliction. It is a sacrament. It is a communion. Will you receive the communion of sickness, of loss of property, of delay, of the withheld completion of desire, of the shattering of an ideal, of the shadow of death? Will you eat this bread, and will you drink this water, joyless and unattractive in itself, as from God's Hand? Will you receive it into yourself, and let it become a part of yourself, incorporate in your selfhood, bone of your bone, flesh of your flesh? Then shall come to pass in you, accepting your adversity and not protesting against it, eating and drinking the sacrament of hardship and not despising the chastening of the Lord,[2] then shall come to pass in your life the opening up of new knowledge,

[1] Heb. ii. 18.   [2] Heb. xii. 5.

the consciousness of new help. "Thine eyes shall see thy teachers, and thine ears shall hear a word behind thee saying, This is the way; walk ye in it."

"Thine eyes shall see thy teachers," — this is the opening of the eyes in the new seeing, which comes only when the sacrament is eaten: that is, when the adversity is accepted as a part of God's gift to one's life. Twice in the Scriptures, in very extraordinary circumstances and in absolutely opposite relations, a new power of vision is represented as following the act of eating, — once in the Garden of Eden,[1] once in the resting-place at Emmaus.[2]

In the Garden of Eden the Devil strove with a human soul to alienate it from the life of God: his point was to make that life eat what God had not offered to it, and his bribe was the promise of a new and godlike vision to follow upon the eating. "In the day ye eat thereof, then your eyes shall be opened and ye shall be as gods, knowing good and evil." The soul accepted from the Devil's hand that which God had forbidden it to accept, and its eyes were opened, but unto what? Unto shame and confusion, and the dread of the Presence of God.

[1] Gen. iii. 7.   [2] St. Lk. xxiv. 31.

In the resting place at Emmaus, in that soft eventide of the blessed Easter Day, there sat at meat a Man and two companions. They did not know Him. He wanted them to know Him. How did He bring it about? "It came to pass as He sat at meat with them, He took bread and blessed it and brake and gave it unto them, and their eyes were opened and they knew Him." "Though the Lord give you the bread of adversity and the water of affliction, thine eyes shall see thy teachers." There are certain lessons we cannot learn until we see our teachers. These are the lessons of adversity. If in the bitterness of our soul we despise the chastening of the Lord, holding the bread and water to be mere prison fare unfit to be eaten, there will be nothing in adversity to teach us; we shall be not one whit wiser, or richer, or grander in character. It is not adversity that sanctifies. It is the acceptance of adversity as a sacrament offered by the Risen Lord. In the acceptance of what He is pleased to offer us, comes the opening of our eyes to see our teachers. For there are certain things which no man can ever learn, which even God Himself cannot teach, except through adversity. There could not be patience without adversity, for patience is the power of suffering calmly some dispensation of the Adversus. There could not be fortitude without adversity, for fortitude is the glorious endurance in the presence of that which brings the strain and the pang and the pressure of the Adversus. There could not be tested faith without adversity, for we have not known the deeper meanings of faith and trust till we have dared to throw ourselves on Christ in an hour of trial, and to enter personally into the fellowship of His sufferings. " Thine eyes shall see thy teachers." Oh, that new seeing which comes like an added sense when one has taken, even once or twice, the communion of hardship from the Hand of Christ, that new sense of the meaning of life when one has suffered even a little for righteousness' sake!

> "Only by its woes
> Our life to fulness grows!"

"And thine ears shall hear a word behind thee, saying, This is the way; walk ye in it." This is the new hearing given to him who takes and eats this bread and drinks this cup, accepting his adversity as a sacramental gift of God. In the hour when he ceases to beat against his fate, in the hour when without bitterness he accepts his portion, there begins to come into his life a sense of the nearness of Christ, and an assurance, nobler in its influence than anything else on earth, that in suffering he is not losing all, but gaining all; and his ears, quickened of God, hear a word behind him, a word of calmness, a word of reassurance, saying: "This is the way, walk thou in it."

"This is the way." Oh, word of comfort indeed! setting us right about the meaning of life. Hardship and trouble seem to him whose eyes are not opened, whose ears are not quickened, like the losing of the path, like a plunge in the darkness over the brink of the path into the thicket and the fen. And he struggles there in the darkness, feeling that his life is broken and overturned. He thinks that he is alone. Others seem to have gone on and left him to struggle in the dark. At last, weary of struggling in a place without a path, he bethinks him of Christ, and in the darkness and the loneliness he wishes that he knew where he might find Him, that Christ would come to him and lead him up to the path once more. He prays, he trusts, he accepts the will of God; and, lo! a gentle whisper in the darkness, a word behind him saying: "*This* is the way; walk thou in it." Christ is there with him, and has never left him. He has not lost his way. *This* is the way, — strangely dark, and strangely rough, and strangely lonely, but still the way that leads out at last into the sunlight. Amen.

XII.
THE SPLENDID IDEAL.

XII.

THE SPLENDID IDEAL.

"That the *Life of Jesus* may be manifested in our mortal flesh."— 2 CORINTHIANS iv. 11, R. V.

THE theme of this sermon is The Splendid Ideal. What else could it be with such a text, so clear, so fearless, so purposeful, so comprehensive? In the realm of the industrial arts, man by thought and skill has realized many wonderful ideals, in bringing resultants of beauty out of unlikely and unbeautiful substances. Out of the lump of dingy ore he coins the glittering eagle and the shining sovereign; out of the bale of unclean rags he brings the reams of spotless paper; out of the black mass of coal tar he evolves the brilliant colors of the rainbow. But the most splendid ideal which ever shot like fire from heaven, to light up man's mind, came when it was given him to conceive of exhibiting in a life limited by sin, enfeebled by infirmity, and given over unto death, the light, the symmetry, the strength, of the one All-Perfect Life. If we did not know that the thought was given him of God, breathed into him, as the breath of a new existence, by the breathings of the Holy Spirit, we should call it a presumptuous and daring ideal. But we know that God has given us this splendid ideal; God Himself has taught us to formulate it, and to look upon it as by no means an impossibility; " That the Life of Jesus may be manifested in our mortal flesh."

Under three divisions of thought we shall study the splendid ideal. The three are comprehended in the text. First, there is the idea of manifesting: " That the Life of Jesus may be manifested." Second, there is the splendid thing to be manifested: " The Life of Jesus." Third, there is the scene of this proposed exhibition of " The Life of Jesus manifested in our mortal flesh." Herein, then, are three clear divisions of thought, — the idea of manifestation; the thing to be manifested; the scene of the proposed manifesting. The idea of manifestation is the highest possible thought man can entertain about himself. The thing here proposed for manifestation is the greatest possible thing that can be manifested. The scene of this proposed manifestation is at once the most unlikely and the most appropriate possible scene for this particular exhibition.

The idea of manifestation is the highest possible thought man can entertain about himself. There are times when a man must think earnestly, and think earnestly about himself. He cannot always continue a stranger to himself. Many of us do not desire to be strangers to ourselves; and often we willingly yet anxiously ponder this question: Why am I here? Why was I sent into the world? What does life really mean to me? If it were possible to hold every one to this question long enough to extort the answer, and the true answer, — the answer, that is, which would represent the exact and literal ideal of the individual who gave it, — it is probable that three answers would include the replies of almost all persons. What does life really mean to me? To escape. What does life really mean to me? To acquire. What does life really mean to me? To manifest.

To escape, to acquire, to manifest. These three are thoughts that men have entertained about themselves; probably most men have had glimmerings of all of these three thoughts at one time or at another time: yet, in the heart of hearts, one or the other of these thoughts is dominant, and gives tone to the life.

What does life really mean to me? To

escape. This is the feeblest of the three replies, and I fear must be looked upon as characteristic of the weakest natures. I say so tenderly, but without hesitation. Life appears to mean, to some, perpetual, lucky escape; always getting out of things just in time to evade responsibility; always managing to turn off the hard work upon some one else; always contriving to slip along in happy heedlessness, smiling or whistling; always well out of sight, cruising on some sunny Galilee, when some one else is being crucified at Jerusalem.

What does life really mean to me? To acquire. This is the robust reply of the average natural man, in the race and bound to win. Clear as to his brain, he sights opportunities far ahead, and crowds on all sail to overtake them. Hot as to his ambition, he has no idea of being left behind in anything he undertakes. Kind as to his heart, he wants the best for those he loves, and, outside of getting it, he knows no vocation. "Have I made, or have I lost?" is the balance in which he weighs the years. How many grand, true-hearted men are in this class! It is not I who say they are in it, they say so themselves: "We are men of business through and through." But God is leading some of them to be this not only, but much more than this, — even to touch with their truest selfhood that plane where the life is more than meat, and the body is more than raiment, and where the meaning of life is more than to acquire.

For there is a higher plane, whether man reach it or not, — a plane where he who asks himself, " What does life really mean to me?" answers with most serious and noble joy, It means to manifest. And what is this word, " to manifest"? It is to express something, to say some word with the lips, or with the pen, or with the pencil, or with the brush, or with the chisel, or with the instrument of music, or with the sword, or with the use of property, or with the force and truth of character, which will honor God, the Power-giver, and which will bless, strengthen, delight, or guide others in the saying of it. Yes, to manifest, to express, to utter something, — the consciousness that one is sent here for this is the highest possible thought man can entertain about himself, and out of it have been born the best attainments ever reached by man or woman: the greatest bravery, the most brilliant talent, the most compelling eloquence of character, the most marvellous influence over youth, the most telling witness-bearing for Jesus Christ. Life in its highest sense signifies not, for such, to escape, not to acquire ; but supremely, to manifest, to utter, to express some God-given power of genius, or courage, or love. And wherever we find the greatest, we find those to whom life's supremest meaning has been to manifest, to say in word or deed what one has been given to say. And those who have walked most gloriously on that plane are those whose names are coupled with the greatness, or the beauty, or the bravery of what they uttered, whether their deeds were material or spiritual. Of such were some we knew in the flesh, and others whom we knew only in the glory of their names and in the immortal earnestness of their works. Of such were Roswell Hitchcock and Mary Brigham, Philip Sheridan and George Peabody, Albert Thorwaldsen and Richard Wagner, Robert Browning and Lacordaire, Elizabeth of Hungary and Savonarola, Saul of Tarsus and John the Baptist. To each and every one of these, and to all who share their spirit, the meaning of life has been first and supremely to manifest, to say a word that has been given, to be a voice crying in the wilderness, or shouting on the battlefield, or pleading from the pulpit, or counselling in the school, or consecrating a fortune, or carving thoughts in marble, or revealing humanity to itself through philosophic music and verse. Wide as were the differences between these lives, they were one in this: to all of them alike life meant more than to escape, — more even than to acquire: it meant supremely, to express, to utter, to manifest that which had been given them, that they might not keep it to themselves, but that they might give it forth again to others. The highest meaning of life for us therefore, as for them, is not to have escaped toil and care, and to have slipped along easily; it is not to have acquired that which satisfies our desires, and which enables us to settle down in comfortable tranquillity: the highest meaning of life is to express, in word and deed, the best which God has made known to us. He who simply escapes has his poor reward; he to whom life only means to acquire has his share of satisfaction if his plans turn out well; but only he who has caught the idea of expressing in his life some word, some thought of helpfulness which God has given him to say, — only he has thought the highest thought which man can think about himself.

As we study onward concerning this splendid ideal, which God sends to our minds through His Word, we find not only that it is an ideal of manifestation, which is the highest possible thought man can entertain about himself, but we find also that the thing here proposed for manifestation is the greatest possible thing that can be manifested. The splendid ideal is not only that we shall live the life of manifestation, as against the ignoble life of mere escaping, or as against the insufficient life of mere acquisition. The splendid ideal is, that in our manifesting, we shall manifest the greatest thing that could possibly be manifested: "That the Life of Jesus may be manifested." There are not two opinions about the grandeur of the Life of Jesus. Whatever men may confess or deny about the Nature of Jesus, all men grant that the Life of Jesus is the most perfect life, in its purity, truth, and love, that has ever been revealed on earth. All men believe in His holiness. Even the devils believe and tremble. Let us speak for a moment of the Life of Jesus, and rest in the brightness of it. What a perfect circle of radiant qualities meet in Him! so that, whatever form of excellence we think of, we find it completely expressed in Him. What holy and entire separation from sin we find in the Life of Jesus! Tempted as He was, in ways so fierce and so frequent, sin could find no door of entrance; the tempter never discovers an unguarded point; he is always driven back. What long-suffering we find in the Life of Jesus! Patient in tribulation, silent under provocation, reviling not again, looking even with large-hearted compassion upon his ignorant murderers, He is indeed the incarnation of long-suffering. What obedience we find in the Life of Jesus! His Father's wish is law unto Him, from the beginning to the end. His meat is to do the will of Him that sent Him, and to finish His work. What sympathy we find in the Life of Jesus! His is the most affectionate and tender of lives, never impatient of the claims of suffering, never repulsed by the offensiveness of disease, most marvellous in His power to understand and minister unto the griefs of the heart, gentle and reverent toward the little children! What submission we find in the Life of Jesus! He has given himself to His work, and He accepts all that comes with it — its loneliness, its humiliation, its terrible pressure, its final and consummating agonies! What steadfastness we find in the Life of Jesus! A glorious, undeviating purpose: whether men walk with Him, or walk with Him no longer; though plots are thickening in His path, and passionate outbursts, premonitory of the bitter end, are breaking forth against Him, — nothing can turn His face, once set towards Jerusalem. Oh, the perfect life! Well did St. John say, "And the Life was the Light of Men."[1]

It is this, it is even this, which is given us, in the splendid ideal, as the thing we are to express, to utter, to manifest: "That the Life of Jesus may be manifested;" that His Life, which was uttered once in the days of the flesh, as the revelation of the Father to men, may be uttered again by each one of us as the manifesting of that same Life to those who are round about us. This is the will of God concerning us. This is God's splendid ideal for us. This was God's splendid ideal for man at the very beginning, when He said, "Let us make man in our image, after our likeness,"[2] and when God created man in His own image. And God never departs from His ideals. Man has become a sinful person, defacing the Divine image. But God has the same splendid ideal for man fallen which He had for man unfallen. And, in Christ, God has taken steps to realize in man the accomplishment of His long postponed ideal by redeeming man, by giving back His Holy Spirit to man, and by creating through that Spirit the desire in man's heart "to be conformed to the image

---

[1] St. Jno. i. 4.   [2] Gen. i. 26, 27.

of His Son,"[1] that the Life of Jesus may be manifested in us and expressed by us. This desire is already created in the hearts of many of us. We are conscious of the splendid ideal, as in a true sense our ideal; and often, in our moments of greatest spiritual elevation, we look forward to a time of immortal completeness, when we shall be rid of these impediments of earthly habit, and these tendencies of earthly sin, and when, standing in the blaze of the Eternal Light, we shall at last attain the splendid ideal, and manifest in our glorified characters the Life of Jesus. We connect this hope with our Resurrection, saying with the Psalmist, "I shall be satisfied, when I awake, with Thy likeness."[2] We connect this hope with the manifesting of Christ in His glory, saying with St. John, "It doth not yet appear what we shall be, but we know that if He is manifested we shall be like Him, for we shall see Him as He is."[3] And so we chiefly look to the future state as the scene of this exhibition of the Life of Jesus in ourselves, the scene where the splendid ideal shall at last be realized.

But this is not the point which is pressed upon our attention in this scripture open before us; this far-off scene of future glory is

[1] Rom. viii. 29.   [2] Ps. xvii. 15.   [3] 1 Jno. iii. 2, R. V.

not the scene to which we are advised to limit the splendid ideal. On the contrary, there remains one part of our text yet to be considered, which brings to the heart a sense of joy and hope. We are told that the scene of this proposed manifestation is at once the most unlikely and the most appropriate scene for such a manifestation. That the Life of Jesus may be manifested, where and when? Not in our immortal spirits after they are delivered from this body of death. Not in that illustrious hour of awaking and of glory when we shall see Him as He is, and when perfectly reflecting His likeness in the mirror of a perfected life, we shall be absolutely conformed to His image; not then, but now, to-day, here: "That the Life of Jesus may be manifested in our mortal flesh." Most unlikely scene for such an exhibition! Our reason would say, "Anywhere but here is the place for a man to manifest in himself the Life of Jesus." In our mortal flesh! our dying flesh! — what pathetic realism in this word! How perfectly uncertain our life is, intensely mortal, subject to death from the hour of birth, liable to be cut off in a day, in a moment, in the tenth part of a second! How subject to the physical infirmities of the mortal state: to pain, with all its ingenious power to torment the nerves and wear out the will; to over-fatigue, with the loss of courage and the lack of self-control which attend upon it; to old age with its decaying faculties! And how compassed about is our mortal flesh with the influence of that of which death is the wages and the offspring, even sin! Sin is in our mortal body, and in our mortal life, through and through. The temptations of our mortal flesh, how terrible they are! The tendencies ungovernable by the will, the base desires of the flesh, the covetous desires of the eye, the unspiritual vainglory of life, — how utterly unlike are these to the Life of Jesus, and how unlikely is such a scene as this of our mortal flesh as a scene in which to express, to manifest, to have our life become an utterance of the Life of Jesus! "Oh, let us be delivered," we cry, "from this body of death; let us put off this mortal flesh and all the infirmities and unholinesses which have attached themselves to us; let us rise to the immortal state, to the Eternal Light, and there we will manifest the Life of Jesus." "Not so," saith the Spirit, "but now is the splendid ideal offered you: that the Life of Jesus may be manifested in your mortal flesh."

And as the Spirit presses the splendid ideal upon us, we think another thought. This life of our mortal flesh may seem a most unlikely scene for the exhibition of the Life of Jesus, but is it not the most appropriate of all possible scenes for such an exhibition? Where ought the Life of Jesus to be manifested and honored if not in that mortal flesh which He took upon Himself that He might endure therein His own humiliation, and share therein our burden and our temptation? "Forasmuch, then, as the children are partakers of flesh and blood, He also Himself likewise took part of the same."[1] It was in our mortal flesh Jesus became Incarnate. It was in our mortal flesh Jesus was tempted. It was in our mortal flesh Jesus groaned in agony, while drops of blood coursed downward to the ground. It was in our mortal flesh Jesus was raised to the Cross, a spectacle of derision before the eyes of the world. It was in our mortal flesh He died and was hidden in the grave. It was in our mortal flesh, changed with the Resurrection change, He rose and ascended up on High, leading Captivity captive, and giving gifts unto men. Is it not right, then, that the Life of Jesus should be expressed, uttered, manifested, here and now, in our mortal flesh? While all things are as they are, — full of confusion, overwork, sinful desire,

[1] Heb. ii. 14.

strain, incompleteness, noise, vanity, sickness, sorrow, change, — this is the splendid ideal which the Holy Spirit gives to every one of us who is also one of His.

It is the splendid ideal for the mother in her home; that, amidst the nameless cares and irritations, the perpetual arrears of unfinished work, the broken rest, the wearied nerves, the Life of Jesus, in its sweet patience, its matchless sympathy, its holy wisdom, may be manifested in her mortal flesh.

It is the splendid ideal for the man of business that, amidst the baseness of unholy minds and the profane wit of unclean imaginations, he may show the purity of Christ's thought in his own; that, amidst the unscrupulous dealers in the rights of others, and the cunning lovers and makers of lies, he may utter the truth and the honor of Jesus in every verbal engagement, in every written promise; that, amidst the free indulgence of intemperate appetites, and the unmanly neglect of home, he may show the simplicity and self-control and chivalry of Jesus. So shall the Life of Jesus be manifested in his mortal flesh.

It is the splendid ideal for those who enter society that, amidst the scenes where conversation is of the lightest, and where by common consent seriousness is out of form, they, if they enter, may show the earnestness and helpfulness of Him Who thought life too great and grand and high, at any time, to close His eyes against its truth.

It is the splendid ideal for the boy in his boyhood that, when the whisperings of dishonor and the invitations of secret wrong are in his ears, he may stand unabashed on the side of Jesus, and dare to be separate from sinners; that, when the unstable wills of others are bending and swaying in the gusts of impulse, he may walk erect in the earnestness of Jesus, and manifest in his mortal flesh the steadfast life of his Great Head-master. Amen.

XIII.

THE MOUNTAIN-CLIMB OF LIFE.

XIII.

THE MOUNTAIN-CLIMB OF LIFE.

PREACHED ON THE FIRST SUNDAY IN THE YEAR 1891.

"Wait on the Lord; be of good courage, and He shall strengthen thine heart: wait, I say, on the Lord." — PSALM xxvii. 14.

ON this first Lord's Day afternoon of the New Year, the sense of the beginning still lingers with us. We are still getting ready to climb the mountain; this Matterhorn of a New Year, which springs from the base, where we are standing, up and up into the silent blue. We are seeing if there is meat and drink in our wallets, against the biting hunger of that upper air; if our staves are well shod with iron, against that slanting sea of glass, up whose billows of ice we shall have to climb: if our guide-ropes are all stout and ready, against the time when none shall dare proceed except he be tied to the bold, experienced Guide Who goes before him.

And there may be time for one more word before we start; one last caution to each mountain-climber, which shall be better to him than the food and drink in his wallet, and better than an iron-shod alpenstock, if he will say it to himself, again and again and again, when the steepness, and the slipperiness, and the solitude, and the space, and the roar of the flying avalanche, and the heart-searching frost made him afraid : " Wait on the Lord ; be of good courage, and He shall strengthen thine heart : wait, I say, on the Lord."

I say, if he will say it to himself. As he climbs the Matterhorn of another year he may or he may not be given the chance to say this to any other soul. If he has the chance to speak this word of courage to another, so much the better for that other and for him : but he must say it to himself ; each must say it for himself to himself, and say it often ; say it to his own soul as if he were speaking it to another: " Wait on the Lord ; wait, I say, on the Lord." In the Psalm, these words are not an address to others, they are the words of the Psalmist speaking to his own soul as he climbs the steep ascent. They are a soliloquy ; a life talking to itself, and telling itself how and where cometh strength into it : " Wait on the Lord ; be of good courage, and He shall strengthen thine heart : wait, I say, on the

Lord." Herein is the strength of these words for us to-day, — that they are a soliloquy; words which we may all speak to ourselves now, and which each one shall need to say to himself many, many times, I believe, before this mountain-climb of the year is over.

What means it, this twice-given reminder to "wait on the Lord"? Do we catch any real point in the word "wait" which is specially strong and suggestive at this particular time? I incline to think that, when we analyze our own conception of the meaning of "Wait on the Lord," many of us do not find anything particularly clear, or particularly suggestive of courage and a strengthened heart. Some may have thought of "Wait on the Lord" as meaning about the same thing as "Wait for the Lord," "be patient;" but that grace of patience, however noble and sweet it is, is not the same as waiting on the Lord; it has not the "action" in it. And some may have thought of waiting on the Lord as simply meaning prayer: "Continue in prayer." But, however grand and true a thought prayer may be, it does not convey that peculiar charm of meaning which is reserved for us in this word "wait," — a meaning which, when Hebrew study first discovered it to me, and ever since, has opened in my life a fresh fountain of joy and strength, and has engraved upon my imagination a picture of aspiring and glorious action. There are eleven different words in the Hebrew tongue which, in our common version of the Old Testament, are translated by the single English equivalent "wait." All shades of meaning which can be attached to "waiting" appear in these eleven words, — the silence of waiting, the earnestness of waiting, the hopefulness of waiting, the watchfulness of waiting, the slavery or servitude of waiting, and others. But when we come to the word קָוָה we find a totally new conception, which leads us far from all these other ideas of waiting; and, indeed, causes us to feel that "wait," as we commonly understand the word, is by no means the most vivid translation of which the Hebrew verb is susceptible. The root of קָוָה means a rope; and the distinctive meaning of the verb is to *tie fast a rope*. The two most conspicuous examples of the use of this particular verb — meaning, "to tie fast a rope" — are, one of them, the text for to-day: "Wait on the Lord; be of good courage, and He shall strengthen thine heart: wait, I say, on the Lord;" and the other is that text in Isaiah which to some of us holds in itself the very essence of life's hope, — " They that wait upon the Lord shall renew their strength; they shall mount up with wings as eagles; they shall run and not be weary, and they shall walk and not faint." [1] If now, instead of using the general and indeterminate word "wait," which is open to many different interpretations, we use the specific expression, "to tie fast a rope" (which gives the distinctive meaning of the Hebrew), behold what a light, behold what a blessed fulness of thought, is created by these two magnificent texts of God's word, — " They that are tied fast to the Lord shall renew their strength; they shall mount up with wings as eagles; they shall run and not be weary, and they shall walk and not faint." "Tie thyself fast to the Lord; be of good courage, and He shall strengthen thine heart; tie thyself, I say, fast to the Lord."

As we utter these words a picture flashes before our eyes, and engraves itself upon the imagination, — the mountain of the Matterhorn in Switzerland, rising in magnificent proportions through chaotic masses of lower hills, and lifting its awful front into the upper atmosphere. On its sides are the broad curve of the glacier track, the jagged darkness of

[1] Isa. xl. 31.

the crevasse, and the glittering billows of the slanting sea of ice. At the base stands a company of travellers and guides, about to begin the ascent. They are making their last inventory of equipments. There are blankets for the shelter, there are wallets filled with meat and drink. There are staves spiked with iron. "Is not this enough?" say the ardent travellers. "Why be burdened with those coils of rope?" And the guides, whose life-training has been upon the ice mountains, answer, with the grave smile of experience, "Travellers, leave behind you, if you choose, blankets, wallets, and staves, and without them you might have dim chance of living to go up; but leave not these ropes, which shall tie us to you, and you to us! There are places yonder where no inexperienced head could bear the dizziness, and no inexperienced heart could surmount the terror, but for the sense of security which this rope shall give, that ties you to your guide. He will go before you and lead you, always upward; the drawing of this rope will itself assure you of the way; the sense that this rope is around his life as well as around your life will brace you with the feeling of companionship, even at that steepest and most awful point where he, being directly above you, cannot be seen. And if you slip, if your foot misses that narrow notch hacked for a footing in the ice, you shall not be dashed to pieces a thousand yards below; he has anticipated that slip, — has thrown his strength upward against the downward drag, and that rope, tightening like a living bond, shall hold you up from death."

So the picture is before us, and each sees, in that glittering peril of the Matterhorn, the steep ascent of life as it rises upward before himself, even from this solemn hour, — up! up! up! through days, and weeks, and months; and each sees in the face of a traveller his own face; and each sees in the strong, earnest, loving face of a Guide the Face of Christ. And the Guide says: "Leave anything behind sooner than that bond with which you can tie yourself fast to Me. Tie fast to Me, and I will strengthen your heart: severed from Me, ye can do nothing."[1] And the Holy Spirit, whispering the thought, which seems like our own thought, enables us to say to ourselves, in most earnest soliloquy, as we look up the steep ascent, "Tie thyself fast to the Lord; be of good courage, and He shall strengthen thine heart: tie thyself, I say, fast to Christ."

[1] St. John xv. 5, margin.

Let us for a moment stand looking up this mountain of life, and consider what it means to be tied fast to Christ, with a bond that encircles our life and encircles His Life, and stretches from Him to us.

It means for us, as for the climber on the Matterhorn, Leadership. If you have ever climbed a steep and dangerous mountain you will understand how nothing is easier than to be bewildered and to lose the way on a perfectly open, treeless mountain. The tremendous angle of elevation prevents you from looking far above you, and the perils which attend every placing of a hand or of a foot demand your eyes and your thought on every foot of ground immediately before your face. What leadership, then, is in the drawing of that rope, as the guide, knowing well his path, turns here and there, and the rope pulls now to right and now to left! You can follow without looking. You do not ask to see the distant scene. While the drawing of that rope continues, "one step enough for you!" Ah, he who ties fast to Christ has that leadership! Life is too steep for us to see far above the point at which we stand, and the needs and perils of the instant compel to a great extent the localization of thought on immediate incidents and decisions, without much length of view. But tied to Christ we are drawn, most marvellously drawn, up the right path; and each step we take, though we can see so little beyond it, is a step in the right direction.

To tie fast to Christ means for us, as for the climber on the Matterhorn, Companionship. We may not see Him, because He is so directly above us; but we hear the Upward Calling, and we feel the Upward Drawing, and the electric current of His Strength flows down into our weakness, and we are of good courage, for He has strengthened our heart. Oh, how mysterious and how precious is that sense of companionship which it becomes possible for us to have with an unseen and absent friend, if we are conscious that one bond of unconquerable remembrance and unity encircles both our lives and reaches from one to the other! We are not alone, — we cannot be alone! Greater even than this is that reassuring truth of Companionship given in hours of peril, of vague depression, of unsupportable fatigue, to those who are tied fast to Christ. Through the comfort of sacraments, and the tender joy of prayer, and the marvellous directness of the Word, and the treasures of memory, there come, as through the guide-rope of the

Alpine climber, bracing assurances from Him Who has gone on ahead.

To tie fast to Christ means for us, as for the climber on the Matterhorn, Rescue. Even he whose face is set upward may make the false step. Benumbed by cold, unbalanced by nervous tension, terrified by stupendous peril, he may set his foot unsteadily in the socket cut for him by his guide. And he may slip! But all is not lost. A strength above his own, and joined to his own, has foreseen and prepared itself for this shock; and the rope is strong enough to bear him, even when hanging in utter dependence. And he who is tied to Christ may in an unguarded hour falter and slip. But all is not lost: "Though he fall, he shall not be utterly cast down."[1] He hangs in utter dependence upon the mercy of Christ; but the bond is strong, and saves him from death, and sets his feet upon the rock once more.

"Be of good courage, and He shall strengthen thine heart."

If the traveller should insist on leaving the guide-rope behind, — should say to the guide, "My staff and my wallet are enough for me; go you on and I will follow," — he might say,

[1] Ps. xxxvii. 24.

indeed, to his own heart, "Be of good courage," but would the words mean much more than emptiness by the side of the perils of the Matterhorn? Would they not rather show that he had no conception of those perils,— no conception of the tests of courage which he must meet? So it seems of those who talk of climbing this dread mystery of years apart from any living bond tying them fast to Jesus Christ, who say to Christ: "Go You on ahead as an Example. I will follow You; but I do not need You, and I will not be tied to You. My staff is enough for me; I will choose my path, and keep up my courage." What do such words show but that they who utter them have failed to comprehend the height of the mountain and the hardness of the way?

Let him who thinks to climb the Matterhorn with no rope tying him to his guide, and who, repudiating that bond, still says to his own heart "Be of good courage," let him count up some of the tests that he must stand in going up the mountain. What are the characteristic tests of courage in the greater efforts of mountain-climbing? There is the loneliness. There is probably no solitude on the earth which under certain circumstances is so crushing and saddening as the solitude in a place of peril on a great mountain. It is indeed awful! Not a bird chirps, not a leaf rustles. You might call and no one would answer you; you might fall and lie groaning, no one would run to you; you might die, no one would bury you. It is a tremendous test of courage. But there is greater loneliness, and more exhausting depression, for those who wander on the Matterhorn of life alone. To some natures, this terrible, hungering loneliness comes most overwhelmingly in the days of youth; and if the young heart be not tied to that only sure Guide, the Lord Jesus Christ, it is likely to lose all courage, and perhaps to go far astray. There is a wonderful passage in one of the letters of Lacordaire which describes, as I have never elsewhere heard it described, that nameless, lonely longing of youth. Every time I read that passage I say to myself: "How true that is! he must have known." He says: " Eighteen years have barely passed over us before we begin to experience longings whose object is neither the flesh, nor love nor ambition; nothing, in short, that can take shape or name. Wandering, whether in lonely solitudes, or amid the splendid streets of great cities, the youth is weighed down by objectless aspiration: he turns from the realities of life as from a prison which stifles his heart; he seeks from all that is vaguest, most uncertain, — from the evening clouds, the autumn winds, the fallen leaves, — sensations which feed while they wound him. But all in vain; the clouds disperse, the winds lull, the leaves decay, without telling him wherefore he suffers, without satisfying his soul. O my soul, why art thou cast down? Hope in God? Yes, it is God; it is the Infinite, stirring in our twenty-year-old hearts, which Christ has touched, but which have carelessly strayed from Him, and in which His precious grace, failing to produce its supernatural influence, now stirs the storm which it alone can lull." [1]

Another peril of the Matterhorn is cold; the silent, deadly, stupefying frost, deadening the brain as with opiates, relaxing the limbs, paralyzing the will, — death to him who is not tied to his guide. Spiritual death to him who is not tied to Jesus Christ, when the coldness and apathy of one's environment strike to the inner being of him who began, in all sincerity, to try for the Upward Life. "Be of good courage," he whispers drowsily to himself; "I can shake this off, and in my will-power rise above it;"

---

[1] S. Lear's *Lacordaire*, p. 30.

and even as he whispers he falls and sleeps the sleep of death. Oh, the warm Strength of Christ! the Vigor of Christ! the irresistible Upwardness of Christ! That only can pull us together, and pull us upward from the languor of a frozen life!

Another peril of the Matterhorn is the altitude. As we enter the greater heights the air grows thin, the pressure augments, the heart pumps like an engine, the lungs draw like furnaces. Oh, what a rest to strain that rope a little, and let him who is used to travelling in this air pull us with his strength! And when the hours come, as they are sure to come, when the pressure of living makes a labor of existence, when the heart is strained to bursting, who knows best what relief is? who has the better chance to escape collapse? — he who only knows how to clench his teeth and pant in desperation to himself, "Be of good courage;" or he who can test the strength of the bond that ties him to Christ, who can draw upon Christ's Strength and Christ's Onwardness, saying to himself, "Be of good courage, and He shall strengthen thine heart"?

Another peril of the Matterhorn is the avalanche. Thunder without lightning; a volley of icy stones; a hissing streak of impacted snow — there! here! there! Gone! All is over, — over before we know what has happened or why, as with a cruel jerk, the guide flung us under the lee of the boulder. But he gently lifts us up, his face all grave and tender, saying, "I saw it coming. It would have killed you. There was nothing for it but to throw you (roughly, perhaps, but quickly) under the shadow of the rock till the avalanche went by." Blessed is he who is tied to Christ when the avalanche comes. Christ will not stop it, nor turn it aside from our path; but He foresees it, and if we are only so joined to Him that He can act upon us, He will draw us into the cleft of the Rock, into the shadow of the mighty Rock, till this calamity is overpast.

Another peril of the Matterhorn is the false step. He cuts the sockets in the ice, and sets His Feet in them. We, clambering after Him, set ours where He set His, till in a dizzy moment the foot is set unsteadily, — slips. Is all over? Shall the shepherds in the springtime find the wreck a thousand yards below? It might have been. God knows it might have been, but for that dear bond that tied us to Him, — that was strong, that held, — and His Strength was made perfect in our weakness.

> "Saviour, where'er Thy steps I see,
> Dauntless, untired, I follow Thee;
> Oh, let Thy Hand support me still,
> And lead me to Thy Holy Hill."

And so we come right back to that point: Tie thyself fast to Christ. Tie thyself, I say, fast to Christ. Then be of good courage, and He shall strengthen thine heart. Severed from Him, courage is bravado, and to essay the mountain is to tempt Providence. Tied to Him by the bands of an unquestioning faith, He will lead thee up, and He will give His Holy Spirit charge concerning thee, to bear thee up in His Hands, lest at any time thou dash thy foot against a stone. Amen.

XIV.

CHRIST'S KNOWLEDGE OF OUR SINCERITY.

XIV.

CHRIST'S KNOWLEDGE OF OUR SINCERITY.

"Thou knowest that I love Thee." — St. John xxi. 17.

The sweetest, strongest thought a man can hold in his heart as he faces life's responsibilities is this: Christ's knowledge of our sincerity. "Thou knowest that I love Thee." It is not good for man to be alone. It is not good because it is not normal. Self-consciousness, the power to know one's self, is but half of personality. The other half is communion, the power to know another in love and trust. He that has never loved has never lived. "He that loveth not, knoweth not God, for God is love."[1]

Love is an expressive function; it implies an object exterior to itself, without which love is inconceivable. Love is potential communion; communion in the wish if not in the fact. Not so ambition: ambition may be strictly self-limited, self-centralized, introactive. The man of

[1] 1 Jno. iv. 8.

ambition may care but for himself; the man of affection is, in the nature of the case, up to his own measure, whatever it may be, an expressive, self-giving life.

Expression is the language of love: it is love's vernacular. But powers and opportunities of expression are variable quantities; may sometimes, in rare, golden hours, be commensurate with that emotion of which they seek to be the vehicles; may oftener, by reason of weakness and fear, be dwarfish and barren; love rising to its highest level of nobleness; expression perversely dwindling to a commonplace.

In such an hour love has still a refuge. Expression has been tried and found wanting. Dumb when it would be all speech; commonplace when it would be glorious; trite, feeble, faulty when it would have uttered the unutterable, — love has still a refuge: "Thou knowest that I love Thee." Rising from earth-bound powers, from stammering and stunted words, from feeble self-justifications, from plaintive apologies, love leaps to its heroic ultimatum: "Thou knowest that I love Thee."

So Simon Peter stood before his Risen Lord; and thrice that awful inquisition tore its way, like a relentless search-light, through the shadows and failures of his life: "Simon, son of Jonas, lovest thou Me?" What could he say? could he appeal to his record, and offer it in evidence as a demonstration of his love? Ah! should he try to speak of this, the memory of his own failures would choke him, the stains on his record would silence him. For he has as his portion a full share of the bitter memories of an undisciplined character; immature professions of fidelity, neutralized over and over again by unbalanced words, by jealous, presumptuous, unspiritual deeds; and upon him is even now the fresh blight of that immeasurable error when, unmanned by excitement, his very life, as he stood in the high priest's palace, had seemed to break up under him, as the ice breaks up in the spring freshet, and, heedless of consequences, lost to honor, he had repudiated his Master in the open presence of men.[1]

Yes, what could he say, as the search-light of the Saviour's inquisition ploughs its way through the shadows of his life: "Simon, son of Jonas, lovest thou Me?" Could he appeal to his companions to speak for him, and testify on his behalf? Had they not known all the weakness of the undisciplined past, — the lapse from faith when called by Jesus to walk on the

[1] St. Jno. xviii. 15-27.

water of the Sea of Galilee;[1] the jealous contention over who should be the greatest;[2] the presumptuous, unseemly rebuke spoken to Jesus at the Last Supper;[3] the drowsy failure in Gethsemane, when the one request of the agonizing Jesus went unheeded, and sleep destroyed the vigil of sympathy for which Christ longed?[4] Had they not known the story of the last desertion, — its desperate, threefold insistence, its cowardice, its profanity?[5] How then could he ask them to testify, when so much in the open story of his life spoke against his love for Jesus?

Yet, in the face of these memories of an undisciplined character which forbade the appeal to his record and the appeal to his friends, this man has still a refuge, for he is a lover of Christ. The Saviour's question does not convict this man of insincerity, however it may convict him of inconsistency and pierce him with penitence. "Lovest thou Me?" The words, in themselves so gentle, are keen as a surgeon's knife, piercing even to the dividing asunder of soul and spirit, and of the joints and marrow, laying bare the thoughts and in-

---

[1] St. Matt. xiv. 28–31.
[2] St. Lk. xxii. 24–31.
[3] St. Jno. xiii. 4–9.
[4] St. Mk. xiv. 37.
[5] St. Mk. xiv. 71.

tents of the heart; but, like the surgeon's knife upon the living subject, the pain they cause shows there is life and not death. "Lovest thou Me?" It is an appeal, not to his record, but to himself; not to his witnesses, but to himself; and the appeal is answered in the depths of the man's self-consciousness. He cannot deny his record; there it stands, fraught with inconsistencies, failures, weakness; he cannot, it may be, overcome the prejudice in the minds of others which these inconsistencies, failures, weaknesses may have excited against him; but in those depths of self-consciousness, where he knows himself as no fellow-man can know him, there is that which meets the question of Jesus, "Lovest thou Me?" with an unfaltering "Yes." How shall he substantiate and prove that love? He cannot prove it from his record, blemished and discolored with many a failure; he cannot prove it from the vouchers of his friends, for they know too well how again and again he has been weighed in the balance of trial and found wanting. He cannot prove it by plaintive attempts to apologize for or to minimize past failures. An intuition tells him that were to weaken, not to strengthen, his case. But, on the other hand, he cannot deny himself; he cannot discredit his own self-consciousness. Within him is that which to the Saviour's question, "Lovest thou Me?" returns an unfaltering "Yes." In his self-consciousness he knows that he loves Christ. And to prove that love he has still one refuge, one appeal left, — the appeal to Him before Whom he now stands face to face, and from Whom has come the question, "Lovest thou Me?" So love leaps to its heroic ultimatum, and discarding arguments, apologies, and refuges of words, appeals to Him "to Whom all hearts are open, all desires known, and from Whom no secrets are hid;" "Thou knowest all things; Thou knowest that I love Thee."

"Thou knowest that I love Thee." It is a blessed hour for the Christian when he realizes that he does possess this last and greatest refuge of love, this final court of appeal: Christ's knowledge of our sincerity. For, as we attempt to live our lives in the world to-day, expressing the best that we know, most of us encounter profound discouragements. We encounter, to a greater or less extent, that prevailing sentiment of modern life which may be called scepticism of character. Scepticism exercises itself by no means exclusively upon God and the Word of God. In an age like this, severely critical and severely competitive, men doubt each other as intuitively as they doubt God, and scepticism of character pervades society. I am sure I simply state a fact, which must have been observed by every person of experience, in stating that this is in no sense a confiding age. The spirit of the world is a spirit of alertness, ready at any instant and in any quarter to ripen into suspicion. Scepticism of character is openly declared by many to be a qualification for success. To be on one's guard against others is become a canon of business. Professions of sincerity are not ranked at a high valuation; and apart from evidence, the name of Christian is not held to guarantee character.

In attempting to live our lives in the world to-day, expressing the best that we know, we encounter the difficulty of making our truest self intelligible to others. There are so many conventional restrictions to prevent the explanation of motives, there is such pressure and haste of living burdening the life of almost every one, there is such a tangled network of opinions lying upon the face of society, it is indeed difficult to make one's self intelligible. Motives which to us are clear as the day are to others dubious or unintelligible; conduct which to us appears to utter one thing, to another appears to utter the opposite; till to explain one's self becomes one of the fine arts of living.

In attempting to live, we are often spoiling our own work by incongruous temper, or incongruous conduct. We misrepresent ourselves oftener than others misrepresent us. It is our own foibles, our own blemishes of temper, our own false steps, which help to make our lives an enigma to others. It is with our own foolish hand the interrogation-point is often dashed in after life's most earnest utterances. These are tremendous discouragements, silencing discouragements. They sometimes shake courage to its foundations; they fill the heart with bitterness and agitation; they scatter the tender uprisings of holy purpose, and throw us back in confusion and sorrow. We feel that others doubt us, look askance at us, point at us behind our backs, or smile with scepticism over our confession of faith in Jesus Christ and our vows of discipleship. And the sting of this bitterness is in the thought that we are discrediting a deeper selfhood which, beneath these variabilities of temper, these inconsistencies of speech and conduct, these futile attempts at self-expression, is after all the greatest and the truest part of us. We know that we are sound at the core; we know that when, through all the shadows of fault and deficiency, Christ's great question, "Lovest thou Me?" searches down into our depths, there is that which gives back the unfaltering answer, "Yes." But can we demonstrate this love so that it will be believed? Can we find anywhere a basis for a new beginning in which our confidence, shaken by failure and misunderstanding, can once more lift itself up into joy? Blessed is he who realizes in such an hour that he still has left love's last and greatest refuge, Christ's knowledge of our sincerity. "Thou knowest that I love Thee." Whatever my own poor, faulty words and ways may say to others, awakening in their minds doubt of my sincerity; whatever the verdict of others may be concerning me; whatever my own memory holds up before me of inconsistency and error, — "Thou knowest that I love Thee."

"Thou knowest all things. Thou knowest that I love Thee." As we dwell upon this answer of Simon Peter to the Risen Lord, some great thoughts come from it and speak to us who are Christians.

It speaks to us of the forgiveness of sins. There is such a thing as a life entering into closest union with the Risen Lord only through the mystery of forgiven sin. That was a wondrous parable spoken by the Master to another Simon; let us hear it: "There was a certain creditor which had two debtors; the one owed five hundred pence, the other fifty, and when they had nothing to pay, he frankly forgave them both. Tell Me, therefore, which of them will love him most? Simon answered and said, I suppose that he, to whom he forgave most. And Jesus said, Thou hast rightly judged."[1] And I suppose that the life which says with deepest meaning, "Thou knowest that I love Thee," the life in which love for Christ is a sentiment so deep it cannot explain itself in words, but can only appeal to Christ's own knowledge of its sincerity, is the life that most fully realizes how it has tried the patience of Christ by the shortcomings of an undisciplined character; how it has disappointed the expectations of Christ by weakness when He wanted strength, by denial when He wanted brave and loving acknowledgment; and how over all its long years of incompleteness Jesus has spread the covering of His forgiveness. Yes, through the mystery and the marvel of the forgiveness of our sins, through His patience, through the sorrow on

[1] St. Lk. vii. 40-50.

His Face as He turns and looks upon us when in the fever of temptation we are denying Him, Jesus knits us to Himself; till, though we still are failing and still are faltering, we become conscious of a love for Him answering His Own, and revealing itself as the deepest and truest thing in our nature.

"Thou knowest that I love Thee." It speaks to us of the true depths of fellowship. "Thou knowest": it is the sweet release from the bondage of verbal explanation. To the stranger we must speak guardedly, lest we say too much or too little; we must explain ourselves, lest he misconstrue our meaning; we must call in our witnesses, lest he doubt our words; we must plead earnestly in our own defence, lest he question our sincerity. To the casual guest we must utter the gracious words of courtesy, lest he think us rude; must fill up the moments with ready speech, lest he call us dull. To Jesus we say, "Thou knowest," and feel that in saying that we have said all. "Thou knowest!" It is the word of perfect understanding; explanations would weaken the eloquence of such love. "Thou knowest!" It is the word of perfect rest. "He will rest in His love."[1] It is the word of the Christian when worn out with fruitless work: "Master, I have

[1] Zeph. iii. 17.

toiled all day, all night, and gained nothing, but Thou knowest that I love Thee." "Thou knowest" is a pillow for an aching head, a cordial for a fainting spirit, a sanctuary for a hunted and frightened heart. Such is the union which a life may realize with the Risen Lord. Not a relationship of bondage, as of master and servant: "Henceforth I call you not servants, for the servant knoweth not what his lord doeth; but I have called you friends, for all things that I have heard of My Father I have made known unto you."[1] Not a relationship of distant, ceremonial worship, but a life of tenderest fellowship, wherein the vicissitudes of days and years do but bind us more closely to that faithful, beloved Friend. We grow old along with Him. He stood by us when we were children, He walked beside us in those freer, lighter days; He walks beside us now, when responsibility like a cross is laid upon us, when weariness is oftener with us, when broader thoughts and larger works are calling us, when thickening clouds of impending storm are piling up before us; with us still, with us always, on and on. And in every new experience, in every new temptation, in hours of strength, in hours of contrition, still we say to Him those same words of the deeper, holier

[1] St. Jno. xv. 15.

fellowship, "Thou knowest all things. Thou knowest that I love Thee."

> "Thou knowest, not alone as God, All-knowing ;
> As Man, our mortal weakness Thou hast proved ;
> On earth, with purest sympathies o'erflowing,
> O Saviour, Thou hast wept and Thou hast loved;
> And love and sorrow still to Thee may come,
> And find a hiding-place, a rest, a home."[1]

"Thou knowest that I love Thee." It speaks to us of Christ's knowledge of our better self. Day by day we struggle to explain ourselves, to live intelligibly, to utter the best that is in us. In vain! short successes alternate with swift failures. The very words and deeds by which we would explain ourselves become in our faulty hands like masks and disguises. The unreality of living grows insupportable. Sometimes it seems as if lives were simply stumbling against one another in the dark, so few understand us, so few do we understand. We appear at our worst in perverse hours when we would have shown our best; we talk commonplaces when we would have spoken the very secrets of God; we wound the friend we sought to help, we grieve the life we sought to cheer. We weep with vexation over days that are mere comedies of errors, or deserts of dulness. The eternal, the glorious relief from all this is Christ's knowledge of

---

[1] Miss Borthwick and Mrs. Findlater.

our better self. Jesus knows. He sees the glorious purpose which by some flash of temper or by some maladroit word we nullified this very morning. He realizes and accepts the heaven-soaring prayer which potentially filled our spirit when, under the drowning surge of weariness, we could pant forth but one breathless ejaculation. He measures the celestial ideal of living, which like a city of gold flashes continually before our ambition, and fails continually before our blundering life. He knows us not only as we are, but as we mean to be.

> "All instincts immature,
> All purposes unsure,
> That weighed not as his work, yet swelled the man's amount;
>
> "Thoughts hardly to be packed
> Into a narrow act ;
> Fancies that broke through language and escaped ;
> All I could never be,
> All men ignored in me, —
> This I was worth to God, Whose wheel the pitcher shaped."[1]

Thou knowest all things ; all the secret of the Father, all the counsel of the Spirit, all the life of angels, all the scrolls of eternity: but of all Thy boundless knowledge, this only gives me courage to come to Thee, and offer Thee this day my faulty life: — O blessed Saviour, "Thou knowest that I love Thee." Amen.

[1] Robert Browning : *Rabbi Ben Ezra.*

XV.
THE RETROSPECT OF TRIAL.

XV.

THE RETROSPECT OF TRIAL.

"O thou of little faith, wherefore didst thou doubt?" — St. Matthew xiv. 31.

THIS is one of those questions which search as with a candle the deep and secret corners of our heart. It is like the still, small voice which came after the earthquake and after the whirlwind. The force of this question is in its afterness. It is retrospective. It looks backward and is a question of fact. It is not prospective and theoretical, an inquiry into the possible causes of doubt, nor a speculation upon the probability that one will act thus and thus under given conditions. This question comes in after the experience and comments upon it, — comes in after we have acted, and asks the reason why. "O thou of little faith, wherefore didst thou doubt?" It is the retrospect of trial. The trial is over; the strain is taken off; the fever is broken; the wind has gone down; the sun has come out; life has righted itself;

Jesus, ever faithful, has kept His word, as He always meant to. And we, always ready to bound up buoyantly when strain is taken off, and to sing joyously the hymns of faith when there is nothing in particular to test faith, — we would be quite ready to leave that dark experience behind, forsaken and forgotten, the doubt, the murmuring, the bitterness of soul, all far out of sight and out of mind; we would be ready to go merrily on in the safety and the sunshine. But He will not let us. He insists that we shall go back and review that experience wherein we faltered and failed; that we shall retrace, in solemn retrospect, that unwelcome hour when being weighed we were found wanting, and being tested we were found unequal to the awful grandeur of the experience which He had permitted us to enter as one of life's great opportunities. He insists on asking, "Why, oh why, in that hard hour, when to have believed would have been so glorious, when not to have doubted Me would have been such an evidence of your trust, why did you doubt?" Am I not right in saying this is one of those questions which search as with a candle the deep and secret corners of our heart?

The force of these reflections will appear if

you will use as an illustration the particular incident in the experience of a human soul long ago which is partly recorded in our text. I shall simply speak of the episode in that stormy night which is entirely associated with the Apostle Peter, and of which the only account that we possess is by the author of the First Gospel. When the disciples, toiling on the boisterous sea, caught sight of the Figure moving toward them through the darkness, very naturally they were terrified. Jesus, to allay their fears, called, up the wind, as He moved toward them, those dear words which have brought comfort to so many hearts: "Be of good cheer; it is I: be not afraid." When Peter heard these words which identified the Saviour, he prepared for himself, with characteristic fearlessness, a new and adventurous experience, not contemplated by any one else in the boat. I cannot but admire (however disappointing was the issue) the readiness with which Peter offered himself as the pioneer of a new experience. I do not see any evidence of boastfulness in his attempt. I see only that fearless originality which does not hesitate to enlist in a new experience, nor to commit one's self to a great risk, merely because the experience and the risk may lie out of the ordinary course of action. The fact that men do not commonly go over vessels' sides, with the hope of walking upon the water, is no good reason for condemning the man who does it, if he is honestly sure that he sees that in Christ which draws him out on this new line. I think more people in this world perish in beaten tracks, and go down with sinking ships, than those who come to grief from bravely striking out alone upon the awful sea where Christ is walking. It is altogether impossible for some natures to comprehend how to others the risk of a course is no conclusive argument against its blessedness, and how the fact that most men do not try to walk on water furnishes no reason why one man may not try.

At all events, he presented himself for the new experience. "Lord, if it be Thou, bid me come unto Thee on the water." And like the echo of his own voice came back Christ's answer to him, "Come!" Many times in His ministry Christ said to men, "Come." But never does it have, for me, quite such a thrill in it as here, when He says to Peter, "Come." Oh, what there is in that word, when you think of it, that "Come" which beckoned a life out upon a path that man's foot had never trodden before; which permitted a life to walk where every step was on a trackless element, over the very abysses of destruction; which led a life beyond the range of all parallel experience, and made it the creator of its own precedents. "Come!" It is the broad-mindedness of Jesus, Who neither sanctions the old because it is old, nor bans the new because it is new, but blesses any path, new or old, that truly leads to Himself. "Come!" It is the sympathy of Jesus, Who can understand every man's life, even the aspirations of him who conceives of doing that which human experience has declared impossible, but which has the glory of Christ as its goal. "Come!" It is the fellowship of Jesus, Who "suffers us to come to Him through the waters," and to stand with Him on depths where our only safety is in clinging to His Hand. Yes! when we consider the mysterious originality of some human experiences, how some are truly called to launch on unbeaten and unfathomed tracks, it is something more than precious to think, as we do to-day, of Christ standing at the farther end of that strange, perilous track, and saying, "Come!" Peter flung himself upon the new experience with the courage of that "Come" ringing in his ears. He stood upon the depths and they opened not under him, and, treading firmly, with his eye fastened on Christ, the green wave bore him as it had been a floor of malachite.

And now what are the three factors which make this picture such a tremendous soul-picture for many of us? First, you see Peter committing himself with the approval of Christ to a certain new experience: "When Peter was come down out of the ship, he walked on the water, to go to Jesus." Second, you see him beginning to feel overpoweringly the strain of his environment. "When he saw the wind boisterous, he was afraid." His was indeed a terrible situation at the moment, and when he began to consider it, when he lost that highly sustained concentration of his thoughts upon Christ, and began instead to measure the peril of his environment, the strain became overpowering, and he sank to the level of a commoner life, the heroism of a magnificent conception was quenched in human terror, — " he was afraid." And third, you see, reading between the lines of Christ's question, that Peter, faltering then, lost unconsciously one of the most splendid opportunities of a lifetime. "O thou of little faith, wherefore didst thou doubt?" Catch the unspeakable regret and sorrow in the Saviour's tone: "O thou of little faith, why did you do it? Why did you miss your opportunity? I permitted you to come into this experience, that you might have the most splendid opening for heroic concentration ever offered to you. I said 'Come,' that in this awful hour you might unlock the door to a larger life. Why have you spoiled it all? O thou of little faith, wherefore didst thou doubt?" My friend, suppose you had been standing by Thorwaldsen when he was fashioning his statue of St. John; suppose you had seen him, full of his heroical idealism, complete the noble form, and then attempt to put upon the face that marvellous upward look. He tries and fails. He tries again and almost attains. Give him an hour more and he will have it. Alas! he falters, he is discouraged, an ignoble petulance conquers him; he seizes the mallet and breaks the statue in pieces. Had this really been and had you really seen this, would you not have cried with bitter pain, " O thou of little faith, wherefore didst thou doubt? Wherefore didst thou falter at the supreme verge of victory? Wherefore basely miss the success of a lifetime?" So, I think, Christ cried out when Peter missed that one supreme moment of concentration and continuance which would have brought the victory. I think Christ sorrowed over him, as He sorrows over every one of us, when, permitted to reach some crucial hour of experience in which fidelity and faith will really count for something almost if not quite sublime, we yield to the strain of our environment, and destroy in fear our most immortal opportunity. I do not doubt that there may come days, yes, hours, in a human experience, when to have endured without murmuring or without doubting, the strain of one's environment, shall permanently elevate character, and set to glorious music all the later years.

"Wherefore didst thou doubt?" These intense, reproachful, sorrowing words of Jesus have power, when we take them to ourselves, and fancy them spoken of ourselves, to start within us trains of thought which, in all their startling individuality, cannot fully be uttered. "Wherefore didst thou doubt?" The retrospection of this question gives to it no small part of its tremendous force. It speaks of the past, and with compelling earnestness forces us to look back and analyze its weakness. It speaks, not of the present, which by some sudden inspiration, some fire-touch of the Holy Ghost, may yet be changed from dulness to glory, but of the past, which has slipped from us and has set itself in unalterable lines. And so the first train of thought it starts, is one which takes us back amidst lost opportunities. It reminds us that one comes, from time to time, to great hours, when the possibility of heroical faithfulness is enormously concentrated; when the far-reaching responsibility of action or of endurance is intensified a hundred fold; when one may live a year in one hour, a lifetime in one day. It reminds us that we may fail to recognize the great meaning of one hour or one day till it has passed us by forever; or that, though conceiving of its greatness, we may falter under the strain of its environment, and not recover till the hour, with its fiery, stormy opportunity, has gone. Thus the Jewish nation failed to recognize her great hour when Jesus came. She stood in her narrowness, killing the prophets and stoning them that were sent unto her, until the hour of possibility was passed and her house was left unto her desolate. How terrible is the sound of Christ's lament over Jerusalem's blindness! "If thou hadst known, even thou, at least in this thy day, the things which belong unto thy peace, but now they are hid from thine eyes."[1] And thus men and women may fail to recognize their great hours, and under the imperious strain of passion, or the rush of fear, or the paroxysm of doubt, may throw away the sublimest things in a lifetime.

There are great hours — great, that is, ac-

[1] St. Lk. xix. 42.

cording to their kind — in many of life's more ambitious pursuits; hours in which the significance of action is immensely great and its consequences immensely long. I have known of men in political life, and of men in financial life, realizing with indescribable vexation, after its departure, that such an hour had been given them, and that through lack of insight or through lack of nerve they had failed to grasp its meaning. To one in whose estimation the making of character and the service of Jesus are the supreme ends of living, how bitter and how absolutely unavailing is it to realize that we have passed in dull unconsciousness, or that we have destroyed through fear and doubt, one of our greater hours, one of our larger opportunities to ennoble character and to serve Jesus Christ! Ah, how easy it is to see the greatness of certain hours in the clear, cold light of sad retrospection! How easy it is to measure the magnificence of possibilities when they have forever passed beyond our reach! We cannot go back to them, cannot live them through a second time. They are lost. In vain we upbraid ourselves. Why did I doubt? Why did I yield to passion? Why could I not have watched with Christ one hour? The Great Hour flashes back upon us its silent, unattainable, impossible beauty, and Christ says to us, "If thou hadst known, even thou, at least in this thy day, the things which belong unto thy peace, but now they are hid from thine eyes."

Another train of thought which is instantly started when one takes these words of the text home to one's self has its rise in that "Come" which Jesus speaks to Peter. That "Come" is a permission, rather than a command. Peter got the experience planned for himself, and Christ let him drop into it, knowing how much more there was in it than Peter counted on, how terrible would be the strain of it. Was it unkind of Christ to permit him? — to say "Come" when He might as well have said "Come not"? I think not. It was severe. But only because, sooner or later, life must be severe, and in the world we must have pressure. If we have or have had our hard times, do not let us forget how much we had to do in planning the course which has unexpectedly developed such terrific depths. We wanted to walk the water, and Christ said "Come," knowing all the while the water was deep enough to drown us. It was not unkind. It had to be. This is life, to take contracts which may be far too large for us; to step out beyond our depth. For thus only comes the possibility of great and crucial hours, great because they are terrible, terrible because they are great. Do I hear some one deny this? Do I hear some sedate philosopher declare, "Strain is unnecessary; it is the result of wild choices; it ought not to be allowed, people ought to have the sense not to get beyond their depth"? My friend, wait. Your turn will come. Your turn will come. You have sailed pretty cleverly, but some day your swelling sails of complacency will have to come down with a run, and you also will go about and lie to, to ride out a gale like the rest of us. Yes! the great "Come" of Jesus permits these experiences which constitute, whether we know it or know it not, our Great Hours.

By what sign shall we know these Great Hours? By the sign of the Cross. They come to an intellectual mind in the progress of the life of faith. You have been living for some time in unusual peace, breathing the serene atmosphere of souls whose faith is stronger than your own. Suddenly the wind changes, and a blast out of the bitter north lowers the temperature of the soul. What is it? It is a new book you have read which trains a new gun of agnosticism against the battlements of faith. It is a new friend you have met, whose sneer at

Christ is sheathed in the velvet of beauteous and seducing words. And the chill of the bitter wind falls upon you, and freezes the Peace of Christ within you. Remember, friend, these are your Great Hours. By the sign of the Cross you shall know them.

They come to sensitive natures in the rude wrestling match with this hard-handed world. A buffet from one you had called a friend; a cruel slight from the hand that erst rested on your own in warmest clasp; a supercilious sneer; a barbed jest shot from the full quiver of some social satirist; a slander dropped like a blot from the pen of some heedless letter-writer, yet staining ineffaceably the page on which it falls, — have such, or any such, come to you? Remember, friend, these are your Great Hours. By the sign of the Cross you shall know them.

They come to impetuous natures in the hour of intense temptation. When the blood is leaping through the veins like a torrent let loose upon the hills; when the imagination is white-hot and sensitive as an uncovered nerve; when the din of passion is beating into the background every caution, every counsel, every command of Christ, — have you lived through this? Remember, friend, these are your Great Hours. By the sign of the Cross you shall know them.

They come to the bursting heart of love when it looks on the suffering of its beloved, powerless to help. When fever is burning up the sweet structure of our most precious hopes; when cries of anguish and sobs of speechless appeal are issuing from lips that we have pressed a thousand times; when Death, like a soulless sculptor, is moulding the altered features into the unworldly beauty of the final sleep, — have you lived through this? Remember, friend, these were your Great Hours. By the sign of the Cross you shall know them.

They will come to the awe-stricken spirits of us all, as, each in his turn, we shall gird ourselves for mortal suffering and prepare for the peril of death. Then, when the way before us changes from the familiar path of health and business to the trackless, sighing wave; when the ship-load of kindred hearts must be forsaken, and the pilgrim of the deep must stand alone to join the beckoning Lord — then shall be our Great Hour. By the sign of the Cross we shall know it.

But there is another train of thought that starts from these words, and leads along the Ascension Path of Christ to that Life from whose heights we shall look back on the Great Hours of earth. It no longer becomes difficult to imagine that that Life must be sublimely happy for all who have known their Great Hours on earth and have lived up to them. When the child whom we thought to be dying sits at our table once again, brown with sunny health, what bliss it is to remember that in the darkest hours of the illness we breathed out to God our deepest belief in His wisdom and His love! When the full assurance of spiritual faith is put into our hands like an overflowing cup, what grandeur is in the memory that, amidst the most sterile wastes of a sceptical environment, we denied not the Blessed Lord! When the friend whose long silence was unaccounted for speaks again the same, deep, changeless word of faithfulness, how peaceful is the joy of remembering that we believed when belief was all we had! And when the Life of Faith is ended and the Life of Sight begins; when we see as we are seen, and know as we are known; when the stone is rolled away from all hidden things, and the buried mysteries believed in and hoped for troop out into the light, — will not Joy's coronet of joy be to remember that when all was darkest and stormiest, we walked on the moving waters with nothing to guide us, nothing to uphold us but faith in Him Who had appeared to us in the storm, and Who had said to our adventurous spirit "Come"? Amen.

XVI.

THE FAITHFUL COMPANION.

XVI.

THE FAITHFUL COMPANION.

"And yet I am not alone." — St. John xvi. 32.

The theme of our discourse is The Faithful Companion. As Christ, amidst the toils and sorrows of His laborious ministry, was continually revived by the companionship of the Eternal Father, insomuch that He could say to His dearest earthly friends, "Ye shall be scattered, every man to his own, and shall leave Me alone, and yet I am not alone, for the Father is with Me," so we, who by faith have known that Blessed Saviour, are permitted to enjoy His companionship amidst the trying solitariness of personal experience, and can say in life's loneliest hour, "And yet I am not alone."

We enter our theme through those opening words, "and yet." They are words of wondrous, pathetic eloquence. More properly we should speak of them as one word. In the Greek there is but one word, the simple conjunction, $\varkappa\alpha\iota$ — "and." But it is invested, by reason of the emotion in the speaker's heart, with a special significance, which is described in the technical language of Greek syntax as the force of "rhetorical emphasis." Instead of being a mere ordinary conjunction, connecting two clauses of speech without reflecting the substance of those clauses, there is injected into it, from the burning heart of the speaker, the fire, the passion of a contrast, an affecting contrast, which the speaker realizes with deep emotion: "And yet I am not alone." This emotional use of the conjunction, by which it becomes the expression of an affecting contrast, has become, to all of us, a familiar form of daily speech. For life is one tissue of amazing contrasts and thrilling surprises: the unexpected is forever happening; resultant facts are continually contradicting probabilities. We are always recording contrasts; always finding life other than it seemed likely to be; always readjusting things with our one word, "and yet," which can be spoken in all tones, from a song to a groan. Who has not said such words as these: "It was such a precious, beautiful life, so needed on earth, and yet God has taken it away." "He seems to have everything that heart could wish, and yet he is so restless and unhappy." "She has so much to worry and depress her, and yet she is so steadfast and strong." "It was such a true, inspiring friendship, and yet the friends are thrust apart." "He seems such a lover of truth, and yet he refuses to believe that Jesus is Divine." "I have no wit or wisdom to see the path before me, and yet God keeps me calm."

Christ, when on earth, seems to have been impressed with the fact that life is a tissue of contrasts, and the special use of the conjunction, of which an example is afforded in our text, is very frequently found in those of His sayings recorded by St. John, such for example as these: "I told you, and yet ye believed not."[1] "I honor My Father, and yet ye do dishonor Me."[2] "We speak that we do know and testify that we have seen, and yet ye receive not our witness."[3] "Have not I chosen you twelve, and yet one of you is a devil?"[4] "Did not Moses give you the law, and yet none of you keepeth the law?"[5] Generally, as these quotations indicate, He was remarking that life does not come up to the level of its possibilities, and constantly contradicts its antecedent probabilities. But our text is a great, a joyous ex-

---

[1] St. Jno. x. 25.
[2] St. Jno. viii. 49.
[3] St. Jno. iii. 11.
[4] St. Jno. vi. 70.
[5] St. Jno. vii. 19.

ception to the prevailing sadness of the utterances just quoted. He is speaking of the loneliness of His Personal Experience, — a loneliness shortly to be intensified by the desertion of His followers. He has drawn a dark picture of that approaching, that impending desertion: "Behold, the hour cometh, yea is now come, that ye shall be scattered, every man to his own, and shall leave Me alone;" when suddenly, like a broad bar of golden sunshine thrust out through the purple folds of an impending cloud, He utters that wondrous "conjunction of rhetorical emphasis," that symbol of contrast between the darkness of that which might be expected, and the brightness, the peace, the comfort of that which actually is: "Ye shall leave Me alone; and yet, and yet, I am not alone, for the Father is with Me."

It is possible to realize in some slight degree the meaning which these words had for the Heart of Jesus. "And yet I am not alone." When we reflect for a moment upon the loneliness of Christ's Personal Experience in the days of His bodily sojourning upon the earth, we pass by such an obvious cause of loneliness as the fact that in manhood He to Whom a home would have been, as it is to us, a haven of rest, had no home; that, whilst the humbler creatures of nature, the foxes and the birds, had their burrows and their nests, He, the Son of Man" (to use His Own words), "had not where to lay His Head."[1] We turn to those more profound conditions which, by their keener edge, wounded more terribly His suffering Spirit, and darkened His Personal Experience with the sorrow of loneliness. The insensibility of Israel and the blindness of the world made His daily path a path of intense loneliness. Twice does St. John use this pathetic conjunction of rhetorical emphasis in dwelling upon this idea. "He was in the world," he says, "and the world was made by Him, and yet the world knew Him not."[2] "He came unto His Own, and yet His Own received Him not."[3] Have we not faculties which to some imperfect extent permit us to realize how the insensibility of Israel and the blindness of the world thrust continually into Christ's affectionate and desiring Heart the anguish of loneliness? Coming to the world with no other purpose than to redeem the world from death unto life, to make its griefs His Own, to toil under the burdens of men, to guide with brotherly counsels men's stumbling feet into

---

[1] St. Matt. viii. 20. [2] St. Jno. i. 10.
[3] St. Jno. i. 11.

the way of peace, He found Himself not wanted and not tolerated — " despised and rejected of men." [1] Coming to Israel as its Prince and Saviour, the Incarnate Fulfilment of all that the prophets had spoken from the beginning, He is met with the cry of inveterate enmity, " We will not have this man to reign over us." [2] With this the attitude of Israel and of the world, His pathway, as far as it touches Israel and the world, must be a lonely pathway.

But the loneliness of His personal experience is intensified by the desertion of His friends. " Ye shall be scattered and shall leave Me alone." He predicted this before it occurred, and the knowledge of its approach made Him conscious always that at the last His friends would fail Him and fall away. Thus, whatever may have been His natural craving for their support, in His Heart He knew that He was their Supporter and they not His. But above all else, Christ's wondrous, unique nature, with its perfect antipathy to all sin, yet living in a sinful environment; with its supreme insight into the thought-life of others, yet detecting there mainly ignorance and unbelief; with its infinite capacity for suffering met by an infinite

---

[1] Isa. liii. 3.   [2] St. Lk. xix. 14.

need that He should suffer, — this, His unique nature, placed Him in an experience where, however intensely human love might wish to bear Him company, human incapacity prevented companionship. His sorrow no human friend could share. Being Who and What He was, He had no choice but to tread the winepress alone. Thus we think our way, my friends, in some true though imperfect degree, into the loneliness of our Lord's Personal Experience, and just as we begin in a sense to grasp it, and just as we begin to say, "Was ever sorrow like unto His sorrow?" suddenly He breaks in upon our thought with that marvellous word of contrast, "and yet, — and yet," with all the loneliness that you can understand, and with all the loneliness beyond that loneliness which you cannot possibly understand, "and yet I am not alone, for the Father is with Me."

If this is Christ's testimony, given in the days when He was walking here in the same world where we are now walking, may not His disciples give in their own way a testimony like His? If He, amidst the toils and sorrows of His laborious ministry, was continually revived by the Companionship of the Eternal Father, are not we, who by faith have known that Blessed Saviour, permitted to enjoy His

Companionship amidst the trying solitariness of our personal experience, and to say in life's loneliest hour, "And yet I am not alone"?

The experience of loneliness is one of the most complex of our experiences; it is found in many a life where its presence is least suspected; it is often produced to an extreme degree in those who have little time to be alone; and although we cannot believe that our loneliness ever approximates to that felt by our Lord, it is nevertheless one of the deepest notes that are ever sounded in our hearts. Having just spoken of the loneliness of Christ's Personal Experience and of the blessed relief which He had in it all, through realizing the Companionship of the Father, I propose further to speak of the conditions frequently encountered in one and another human life where the loneliness of personal experience may be most keenly felt, and where, to those who possess a true faith, the Presence of Christ, the Faithful Companion, will be particularly strengthening.

"And yet I am not alone!" Happy is he who can speak thus concerning the Presence of Christ amidst the loneliness of inexperience. What is more lonely than thoughtful youth? Some natures in the days of their youth make a jest of living; they view every question from the standpoint of a joke; they make the sweetest and the greatest matters trivial by their method of handling them. To such, inexperience has no loneliness in youth; perchance it shall beget a very bitter loneliness ere many years have passed. But to the thoughtful, walking out from their childhood into the wide, wide world of living and deciding and doing; beset at every point with new questions, loaded with new responsibilities, thrilled with new feelings, sensitively conscious that the heart is unskilled, the judgment undeveloped, — to such the loneliness of inexperience is a great reality. We are accustomed to talk in broad abstractions about the sunny freedom of youth; and it is, in many things, a sunny freedom. Yet I question whether any tears we ever shed in riper years are more scalding than some which youth has shed; I question whether the fear of living has ever come with more sickening insistence to any than to some yet trembling on the threshold of life; I question whether any loneliness has created a sense of more utter desolation than in some tender hearts forced by circumstances to stand alone in youth. Happy are they, yes and safe are they, who amidst that prostrating loneliness of inexperience are able to say, realizing the Presence of Christ, "and yet — and yet, I am not alone." To be able to say that is to acknowledge that we have found a Friend, a Faithful Companion, Who will not despise our inexperience, Who will not deride our mistakes, Who will not frown on our youthful desires. It is impossible for me to express the tenderness with which my heart goes forth to inexperienced and thoughtful youth; how great its affairs seem to me; how sacred its aspirations; how pathetic its sadness and its fears. But could I condense all my sympathies with youth into one single expression, it would be to tell the young heart, in its mysterious loneliness, that there is One Friend and One alone Who can take that loneliness away.

"And yet I am not alone." Happy is he who can speak thus concerning the Presence of Christ amidst the loneliness of temptation. There are some of our temptations which contemplate, in their consummation, an open act; there are others which look to consummation in secret deed. Of both forms it may be said with equal truth that loneliness is the final characteristic of temptation. For in the last analysis of temptation, we find the place of decision was in the loneliness of the heart.

There, where the evil desires are caged like unclean birds, where the imagination exhibits its false ideals of the satisfaction of sinning; there, where thoughts utter themselves unabashed whose faintest whisper we would suppress from the hearing of human ears, — thither within himself the man withdraws, willing to indulge himself with unholy solitude; closing in the blinds about the windows of his life; shutting and locking the doors behind him; consenting to ponder evil. God send to such a man in such a moment the startling thought, "And yet I am not alone!" God make such a man suddenly conscious of a Presence with him in what he thought his solitude; God cause such a man to start up and see at his right hand the Holy Saviour, gazing with Eyes where sternness and love contend, and saying, "Arise! Thou art not alone. I forbid thee to bring this shame upon thy soul."

"And yet I am not alone." Happy is he who can speak thus concerning the Presence of Christ amidst the loneliness of spiritual desire. Sooner or later, he who truly leads the life of spiritual desire will find it in some things a lonely life. If any one who believes Christ, with all his heart gives himself up to the longing for likeness to Christ, which is holiness; for oneness with Christ, which is power; for the vision of Christ, which is knowledge, — he must expect to be often in loneliness as far as human companionship goes. This loneliness he will sometimes realize most keenly when all around him are the gay and laughing faces of his friends; when human voices are sounding in his ears like the sound of many waters; when people are jostling and thronging him in the crowded path; lonelier often in the tumultuous and exciting city, where men are, than when standing afar on the white sands of the deserted coast, or climbing, amidst mountain sheep, some voiceless and mist-bound mountain top. The life of spiritual desire is not the life of the world; to prefer it is to prefer what few count desirable; to live that life is to think as the majority do not think. The price of living it is loneliness; it is to know that many think you different, that some think you foolish; it is to realize that your sentiments are the sentiments of the minority; and that if you are lonely you cannot expect much sympathy from your friends. It is a fair question: "Is the life worth the loneliness?" I do not profess to answer the question; but some could answer it who, knowing to its full extent that form of loneliness, have also known all that can come in that loneliness to make one cry out with a joy that is like no other joy, "And yet I am not alone!"

"And yet I am not alone." Happy is he who can speak thus concerning the Presence of Christ amidst the loneliness of advancing years. I do not speak only of old age. Of its peculiar experiences I know nothing save as they have been communicated to me by the aged. Those communications convince me that what I am about to say will be realized as true by all who are older, as well as by many who are younger, than myself. Advancing years are the portion of all of us. Years advance for us all. And in their advance they bring startling changes, — changes, many of them, startling by reason of their suddenness; and many of them no less startling because they have come slowly. For from time to time we arise astonished, and as it were take inventories of the changes in others and in ourselves. We reckon them up in altered countenances, in added stature, in whiter hair, in feebler steps; we reckon them up in the changes of residence and the history of those changes; in new homes founded, in old homes broken up or breaking. We reckon them up in empty cribs, and vacant chairs; in the sudden translation of glorious friends; in mounds, small and great, where buried treasures lie. We reckon them up in life lessons learned, of patience, of obedience, of renunciation, of silence. And in these involuntary inventories of changes, how keenly at times we feel the loneliness of advancing years! How many feel it who are not old, or nearly old! How many who now hear me have been led, through changes, to appreciate loneliness on earth; to realize the necessity for a blessed, enduring life beyond the grave! How many have thought out in substance, if they have not also breathed out in words, those matchless stanzas of Montgomery: —

> "Friend after friend departs;
> Who hath not lost a friend?
> There is no union here of hearts
> That finds not here an end.
> Were this frail world our only rest,
> Living or dying, none were blest.
>
> "Beyond the flight of Time,
> Beyond this vale of death,
> There surely is some blessed clime,
> Where life is not a breath,
> Nor life's affections transient fire
> Whose sparks fly upward to expire."

Against that inevitable loneliness of advancing years it is vain to protest. No human hand can stay that tide, rising steadily over dear landmarks of our life. What strange second-meaning follows like an echo those great words, "We shall not all sleep, but we shall all be changed"![1] Happy they who through the flux of years can know, clearly and yet more clearly, by His very contrast with our life, the Changeless One, the Faithful Companion, Jesus Christ, the same yesterday, to-day, and forever! Then may the waves swing far apart the life-boats toiling towards the shore, and yet we are not alone.

"And yet I am not alone!" Happy shall he be who can speak thus concerning the Presence of Christ amidst the loneliness of death. None but the dead know all the loneliness of dying. The dormant, stolid nature, that has been content to live alone, may not keenly feel it lonely to die. But he who has loved love, whose heart has answered to it as the wind-harp answers to the breeze, — he will find it lonely and strange to die. To the verge of that experience Human Love will attend us; her arms will clasp like the Everlasting Arms beneath our fainting head; when hearing is gone, her eyes will look speechless messages of courage; when sight is gone, her hand will speak by silent pressure. But there is a moment beyond which we must walk alone. Alone? Ah! need it be alone? May

[1] 1 Cor. xv. 51.

we not trust that He Who was before all will likewise come after all, to speak through the senses of the soul, deathless in the dying body? May we not trust that whosoever liveth and believeth in Him shall not suffer the loneliness of death; that the last surprise on earth, the first in heaven, is this: " And yet I am not alone " ? Amen.

XVII.
FORBEARANCE.

XVII.

FORBEARANCE.

"Suffer it to be so now." — St. Matthew iii. 15.

I wish to speak about Forbearance, as one of those elements of goodness and completeness for which we are certain to find plenty of use in the daily round of life, and concerning which Christ has given us both His most beautiful precept and His most Holy Example. The words of our text, when understood, — that is, when seen in the light of what they must have meant to Christ Who spoke them, — are simply perfect as the law and language of forbearance; we might search all literature, but in vain, to find anything so tender, so gentle, so strong, so patient, so grandly expectant, as this word: "Suffer it to be so now." If we saw no more in it than the fact that it is the first official utterance of Christ, it would be enough to rivet our attention. Till now, from His birth, Jesus has been preparing for His official ministry. Thirty years have passed in seclusion, in growing up to the point where, as a Man, He shall take up His public work. And when he begins, behold the quietness of the Beginning! No proclamation of Himself, of His intentions, His claims. No brilliant burst of oratory, announcing that a new star had arisen, a new prophet dawned upon the scene. Instead of this, which had it come would not have been unfitting, the first official word of Jesus is the quiet, gentle, melodious doctrine of forbearance: "Suffer it to be so now."

But let us look into the profounder meaning of the sentence. The circumstance calling it forth we know very well. We remember how the mystic forerunner, the brilliant cousin of our Lord, St. John the Baptist, was fulfilling his severe mission. Young, vigorous, perfectly disciplined, absolutely fearless, with a grand and thrilling voice, with flashing eyes, with hand outstretched and tense as if grasping the very sword of judgment, the Baptizer, the Prophet of Repentance, proclaimed the kingdom of God. Unterrified by menace, undismayed by scorn, he summoned all men to repentance, flinging in the face of Scribes and Pharisees epithets that stung like the viper's fangs, creating a reign of terror in the hardened hearts of soldiers and publicans. By what stroke of mysterious power is this invincible man suddenly broken down? The fire is quenched from his eyes, the tense muscles relax, the ringing voice is broken as with tears, and he, who one moment since was urging and commanding every one to come and be immersed, is now making feeble gestures of prohibition, as if he would keep from entering the water a Man, young as himself, Who has just approached. Before that Man he breaks as under a stroke from heaven, — pain, protest, impatience, struggle in his face, — and in broken words he says: "I have need to be baptized of Thee, and comest Thou to me!" Intuition had revealed to him the Personality that now for the first time he beheld, and before the Incarnation of Holiness, Truth, Wisdom, and Power, for which the ages had waited, he felt his own ministry shrivelled up into nothing; and the thought of subjecting the sinless Christ to a baptism administered by his sinful hands — a baptism that had no meaning save the washing away of sins — was to him intolerable, a false position, an insufferable humiliation of his own spirit. Can we not understand this, who have ever had come to us for help lives that we felt to be infinitely purer, nobler, nearer to God than our own, — souls that could do, nay that were doing, for us more than we could ever do for them? Has not our involuntary sense of truth revealed to us their power, so far beyond our own, and extorted the silent cry: "I have need to be baptized of thee, and comest thou to me!" Their eyes meet, the two marvellous children of prophecy, nurtured apart, and now brought together at the Jordan-side of discipline. They know each other now with a perfect comprehension, and Christ's intensely earnest and quiet word to him is: "Suffer it to be so now, for thus it becometh us to fulfil all righteousness." It was enough. "Then he suffered Him." Protest knelt in obedience, and the disciplined life did for Another what it craved might have come to itself.

But in the words of Jesus, "Suffer it to be so now," far deeper meaning is there than that which applies to John. Think of the humiliation of the baptism of repentance for the sinless Saviour; think of the yoke to which, so quietly and gently, He was then bowing His neck; think of the forbearance of that Heart which could go so meekly in among sinners, and take part in the ordinance which implied and signified sin! How revolting to us is the insinuation of a sin of which we are truly innocent! How infinitely more painful to the absolutely perfect Soul of Christ must have been the freezing shock of that baptism for sin! Yes, He was speaking to Himself in that hour as well as to His friend when He said: "Suffer it to be so now." For these dear and gentle words were the law of His Life from the Childhood to the sepulchre; always suffering it to be as it was then and there; because in that forbearance, that refraining from the assertion of His Own Divine rights, that quietude of spirit and language and action, He was fulfilling His mission of eternal strength, and was opening a way by His Example for the encouragement of all who love Him, and who are finding out every day in their own daily round how often forbearance is the one thing needful; how many, many things in life, in character, they must suffer to be so now, if they ever hope or expect to show forth the Spirit of Jesus in a manner that shall lead others to reverence Him.

Placing, then, clearly before us the great example of Him concerning Whose forbearance Isaiah prophesied, "He is brought as a lamb to the slaughter, and as a sheep before her shearers is dumb, so He openeth not His mouth,"[1]

[1] Isa. liii. 7.

and of whom St. Peter wrote, "When He was reviled, He reviled not again; when He suffered, He threatened not,"[1] I wish to speak of some matters not unworthy to be connected with the Example and Spirit of Jesus. And I do specially connect them with Him, that those just thoughtfully beginning a Christian life, and not sure of what matters may properly be connected with it, may see how, if any one has given himself to the Saviour, trusting in the Blood of the Cross for justification, he must make Christ the central Object of the daily round, and live through all common and uncommon experiences with Him in view. And also, I trust, God by His Spirit may greatly bless this thought to all who have been believers for a longer time, so that if our religion has become a formal and professional and theoretical thing, remote from the actual daily round, we may make haste penitently to seek a new deliverance in Christ from this bondage of formal, unmeaning religious habits, and begin living our common, hourly life in the Presence and for the sake of our Lord. This law of "Suffer it to be so now" was not only constantly reappearing in the only absolutely Perfect Life ever lived among men, it has close

[1] 1 Pet. ii. 23.

and constant relations with us. And may I speak, with great directness, of four opportunities, given more or less to all of us, to manifest our reverence for Christ by reverencing His blessed law of forbearance? More or less, according to age, station, and development of the higher nature, the Lord puts into our lives the opportunities of forbearance toward the inexperienced; forbearance toward the unspiritual; forbearance toward the unreasonable; forbearance at home.

Forbearance toward the inexperienced. In life there is nothing that so makes some people strong, self-controlled, rich in thought, as experience, attended with God's blessing. It has done for them more than ever natural endowment did for them. It has admitted them, often by painfully steep and rough ways, into new realms of knowledge; it has educated them in heart and mind; it has added new gifts, apparently, to their lives; and could they, as they stand to-day, clothed in their long and rich robes of experience, be permitted to look back and see themselves as they once stood, weak and shivering and unclothed, on the threshold of life, they would not know themselves, nor believe that ever they were so poorly furnished. But it is true that once they were without experience, crude and unformed in thought, rash in opinion, fickle in choice; perpetual transgressors, perhaps the trial and torment of dear, patient lives now at rest in God. And it is also true that the most enriching experiences of their lives have come to them gradually, unfolding with years, and developing under the long summer growing time of favoring opportunity. Also, some of the influences which have done the largest things for them were of a kind that could not possibly be understood at first, that in the order of nature must remain without significance till the fulness of time had come. To those crowned with the honorable crown of age, the thoughts, opinions, and decisions which early manhood thinks mature must seem most incomplete and ungrown. But there is far more than kindness, there is the Grace of Jesus, in knowing how to understand and make allowance for inexperience; how and when to say of things that from your advanced standpoint you would desire changed, "Suffer it to be so now." It is most terrible and saddening to think of the mistakes of Inexperience, the lifelong burdens that would never have been taken on had there been any sense of consequences; but it is not less terrible to think of the mistakes of Experience when she has forgotten the Saviour's law of forbearance in dealing with the ungrown and the unformed. Oh, if Experience would not so often look down on Inexperience with contempt, or with relentless rebuke! If Experience would not demand from Inexperience an impossible maturity of conviction and preference! If Experience would devote more time and gentle thought to being the friend and companion of Inexperience, entering into its life, putting itself in its place, discerning between the permanent and the transitional in character, between the qualities that constitute the substance of life and the temporary manifestations of incompleteness, concerning which our Lord's great law of patience and love is, "Suffer it to be so now"! Dear little friend! Shall I rebuke you because you cannot understand some things which I, at your age, knew not in the least? because you cannot feel an interest in some things which to me, at your age, were less than nothing? Shall I condemn you because you are fighting more bravely than I the very temptation of my childhood? Shall I look down on you because your opinions on some point do not comprehend elements you could not possibly know? God forbid! Even now, in many things, you are my teacher; in many ways, my helper. And I, if I would help you, must live in your life, and if I would see you grow up a Christian I must wait for you; and that which is ungrown in you I must "suffer it to be so now."

Forbearance toward the unspiritual. By this term I do not mean to describe those who have no sympathy with religious things, no portion even of nominal or inherited faith, no acquaintance with the Christian effort. My thought is of lives that have embraced the form of religion without apparently discerning its spiritual power, that have received the Holy Name, but apparently without coming to any such personal knowledge of Jesus as leads one to wish and struggle for a separateness of life from many incomplete ways in order to be free for a more entire consecration of thought, time, and labor to the Blessed Master. These lives are contented, happy, untroubled in their combination of the church life with the world life; having a love for the church, but a love certainly as strong for all the most distinctively worldly indulgences, and no conception of finding a higher joy by personally renouncing certain self-indulgences as an act of homage to Christ, and as a means of setting themselves more entirely free for His service. Now, on the other hand, there are those to whom the Grace of God (certainly it is this, and not any goodness of their own!) has brought a more advanced conviction in spiritual matters, and they personally have been led to a clearer view of their Lord and His claims, in consequence of which they are strengthened to take a position far higher spiritually as to the renunciation of self-indulgences of various kinds for Christ's sake. To these, blessed of God in being permitted to have clear convictions on some points where the convictions of others are much clouded, there is the strongest need to commend the grace of forbearance as manifested towards those who have not come to the same state of mind, and who make no response to these subjects of consecration. To these, to whom the Lord has given so much light, He seems to say: "Be very gentle towards those who do not see as you do, nor think as you do. The earnestness of consecration may by an unconscious change in an unguarded moment slip into self-righteousness, and that is the death of influence. Remember that you yourself have only had this light and these views a little while, perhaps. How long you felt as others feel, and suffered the old life to carry you where it would! Remember that special mercy you received and are receiving in the influences around you, and that others not only are without those influences, but have many which are unspeakably adverse. Therefore, when they seem to you to be far off from the Ideal, and most deficient in the expression of higher views, heed My Word: Suffer it to be so now, and for yourself go meekly and earnestly forward, trying so to live in and for Me, that My Spirit may be able to work through your life upon others, giving them the light given to you. And some of them may even now be on the verge of decisions from which one condemning word from you would drive them back forever."

Forbearance toward the unreasonable. These are the lives which, in impatient moments we have said, were sent into our paths only to try us. Let us not justify ourselves; let us not pretend that we have always met these lives in the spirit and temper of Jesus. Let us rather think frankly, even if sadly and in self-condemnation, of the many times when we have resented unreasonableness in others. That it was natural from our standpoint to do so, one cannot deny; that it seemed quite impossible from that standpoint to avoid it, one cannot deny. But, alas! the fault lay in our standpoint, which was much too low and altogether selfish. Had we been standing at the standpoint of the Saviour, we would have had a share of His larger knowledge and of His larger sympathy. His larger knowledge would have told us that these unreasonable lives have had their own fountains of bitterness, stricken open it may be by rods held in hands not their own; that they have seen often the blighting of dear hopes; that they were not thus once, — not till after some day of anguish long ago, of which they speak not, when they saw the light of life blown out in a furious storm, or engulfed in a lonely grave. From that day they never were the same. And while I do not say that any trouble gives one a right to be selfish or bitter, and while it may be we, too, have some things in our lives to endure in silence, I do say that the larger sympathy of Jesus makes one forgive and forget to the end the bitterness born of sickness or sorrow, and to "suffer it to be so now."

Forbearance at home. Is there at home some little thing, coming up now and then, to wear upon your calmness; some manifestation from one or another of the family to provoke the bitter word, the resentful act? Child! parent! "Suffer it to be so now." "Now!" As I say that word it sounds to me like a bell tolling from a tower the prophecy of change. "Suffer it to be so now;" put up with many things for love's sake. It will not be always. It may not be long. There are empty sheepfolds on the moors; the sheep are scattered. There are empty homes soon enough, for the children must scatter, and the parents must say "Good-by." While we may — oh, while we may! let us keep together.

> "The hands are such dear hands ;
> They are so full ; they turn at our demands
> So often; they reach out
> With trifles scarcely thought about ;
> So many times they do
> So many things for me, for you,
> If their fond wills mistake,
> We may well bend, not break.
>
> "They are such fond, frail lips
> That speak to us. Pray, if love strips
> Them of discretion many times,
> Or if they speak too slow or quick, such crimes
> We may pass by ; for we may see
> Days not far off when those small words may be
> Held not as slow or quick, or out of place, but dear,
> Because the lips are no more here.
>
> "They are such dear, familiar feet that go
> Along the path with ours, — feet fast or slow
> And trying to keep pace, — if they mistake,
> Or tread upon some flower that we would take

Upon our breast, or bruise some reed
Or crush poor Hope until it bleed,
We may be mute,
Not turning quickly to impute
Grave fault ; for they and we
Have such a little way to go, — can be
Together such a little while along the way, —
We will be patient while we may.

"So many little faults we find !
We see them, for not blind
Is Love. We see them, but if you and I
Perhaps remember them, some by and by
They will not be
Faults then — grave faults — to you and me,
But just odd ways — mistakes, or even less —
Remembrances to bless.
Days change so many things, — yes, hours ;
We see so differently in suns and showers.
Mistaken words to-night
May be so cherished by to-morrow's light
We may be patient ; for we know
There's such a little way to go."

XVIII.

THE RECOGNITION OF DEPARTED GREATNESS.

XVIII.

THE RECOGNITION OF DEPARTED GREATNESS.

PREACHED ON THE BIRTHDAY OF WASHINGTON, FEB. 22, 1891.

"And it came to pass, as they still went on and talked, that, behold, there appeared a chariot of fire and horses of fire and parted them both asunder; and Elijah went up by a whirlwind into heaven. And Elisha saw it, and he cried, My father, my father, the chariot of Israel and the horsemen thereof."— 2 KINGS ii. 11, 12.

ON this historic day I need not tell you that my theme is The Recognition of Departed Greatness. We have heard from the Old Testament the magnificent account of the apotheosis of Elijah.[1] To that account I attempt not to add one word. By his compelling eloquence the unknown narrator has drawn us all into that last journey of the prophet and the pupil, and we have seen the great man rise to take his seat on high among the godlike victors. Yet I may attempt to say what feature in that scene most deeply moves me to-day. It is not the sweet dignity of Elijah as he comes to the

[1] 2 Kings ii. 1–15.

hour of his reward. It is not the extraordinary manner of his translation, amidst the flashing vision of that cloud-like car of light. With stronger attraction than to these, my mind is drawn to him who is left behind, bereft of his hero-master, and stricken with the solemn sense of life's great vocation and his own unfitness to meet it. Yes, it is to the spirit and to the manner of the young Elisha's recognition of departed greatness my mind is drawn to-day with strong enthusiasm and, I trust, with thoughts appropriate to this anniversary, — a day which no true American should carelessly pass by.

In three most admirable ways Elisha, as a young and thoughtful man, shows his recognition of his departed master's greatness. First, in terms of lofty strength, which honor his own intelligence even as they honor the memory of his master, he worthily describes Elijah's influence upon the safety and the destiny of Israel. When the car of light had borne away his hero, the first passionate impulse of that exalted moment was to acknowledge the true greatness of his vanished friend: "My father, my father, the chariot of Israel and the horsemen thereof." The imagery of his words is the instantaneous reflection of the brilliant vision. As in a dream he had seen the hero lifted to the flaming chariot of triumph; even like that impetuous vehicle of light looks, to his mind's eye, the career of his master, sketched at one stroke upon his quickened memory: "My father, my father, the chariot that now bears thee to God is like thine own bright life. So on the breast of thine heroic courage, thine indomitable patriotism, thy burning faith, thou didst bear thy nation onward and upward. My father, my father, the chariot of Israel thou."

Second, Elisha recognizes the greatness of his departed master in the revulsion of feeling toward fear and self-distrust. "He took hold of his own clothes and rent them in two pieces." There are crucial moments, especially in youth, when fear is nobler than courage, and self-distrust is manlier than confidence. Of such moments this was one. In the first passionate moment following the translation, thought, like a tremendous wave, had rushed far up the shore of memory. There it broke, and returning upon himself dragged him, as by an undertow, into the depths of fear. Buried in an agony of self-distrust, he is conscious now only of the discrepancy between the vanished one and himself, — Elijah's life so splendidly developed, his own so immature; Elijah's grasp upon the forces of his time so tenacious and so masterful, his own so uncertain and so weak. Afraid of his own youth, he seizes the mantle from his shoulders and tears it in pieces.

Third, Elisha recognizes the greatness of his departed master in the disposition to identify himself with the sources of his master's power. Ere yet their companionship had terminated, he had shown this disposition by that reverence which is ever one of the most beautiful characteristics youth can exhibit. "Let thy spirit come upon me, according to the portion of a first-born son." So had he prayed. When now he stands on the empty field, no longer the servant of another, but called to work out his own vocation, he is true to his prayer. He has cast upon the ground the fragments of his own mantle in manful self-distrust. Now from the ground he lifts the heaven-fallen mantle of his hero, and with it appropriates the motive, the faith, the godly strength of his hero's life; linking himself henceforth, in grand humility, to the best that had gone before him. And thus, as he turns away from his master's apotheosis, to shoulder the burdens and fight the battles of his own time and place, Elisha suggests to every thoughtful youth what is the true recognition of departed greatness, everywhere and always. It is not the mere formal service of commemoration; it is not the mere honoring of traditional immortality. It is the broad intelligence which can do more than magnify the present; even which can measure the gloriousness of characters that fought the noble fight and won the amaranthine crown in days, it may be, far in advance of our own. It is that wholesome and modest self-distrust, that anxious self-examination, which in the presence of the great departed, hushes each whisper of boastfulness, and penetrates the conscience with holy fear. It is that reverential inquiry into the sources and springs of departed greatness, with a view to availing ourselves of those sources, and drinking at those springs; that, though the great depart, the essence of their greatness may rise again in us. These observations are pertinent not only to the sacred and ancient narrative of Elijah's departure, but to the deathless associations which invest this day with honor in the calendar of the republic.

On this day, one hundred and fifty-nine years ago, in a homestead at Bridges Creek, upon the wooded banks of the Potomac, a charming and winning child was born to Augustine Washington and Mary Ball, his beautiful young wife. It is almost startling to reflect that that fair infant, sleeping and smiling out the summers of his infancy beneath the waving trees on the Virginian river-bank, and learning the athletic sports of his merry boyhood in the sweet meadows of the Rappahannock, a century and a half ago, bears the name which sixty millions of people venerate, the name that still flashes fire at the touch of sound. " My father, my father, the chariot of Israel and the horsemen thereof." Even with the same thought of which that cry was the expression, we think of him to-day, — the Father of the Nation; the Chariot of our Israel; bearing the cause of Liberty onward and upward, on the breast of his heroical courage, his indomitable patriotism, his burning faith. Blest in his birth, blest in his death, "his body is buried in peace, and his name liveth forevermore." And by what a beautiful coincidence of history are we doubly reminded this day of departed greatness! On the eve of the Birthday of Washington, one of the bravest, truest heroes of the later time has been laid in the grave.[1] Henceforward the Burial of Sherman and the Birth of Washington, locked in the coincidence of history, will draw appropriately near to one another two names representing in common forceful character, devotion

[1] General William Tecumseh Sherman, U. S. A., was buried on February 21, 1891.

to duty; valor, magnanimity. And as these two heroes (now, we earnestly hope, made known to one another in a better world), — as these two heroes lead our thoughts to contemplate departed greatness, how quickly do our memories add the names of others who within the last few years have gone over to the Invisible! Whichever way we look, we are made conscious that gifted and broad-minded and valorous and earnest spirits are leaving us, continually leaving us; summoned, we believe, to pursue higher callings in loftier spheres. In every calling great lights are being extinguished and great vacancies are being created. From the bench and the bar, from positions of state, from the army, from the navy, from the realms of finance and of philanthropy, from the world of authorship, from the ministry of Christ, from the schools of fine arts and of medicine, the leaders of a generation are retiring, having done all save to tell us who shall take their places. And what shall we do? Shall we only stand mute with the sense of loss as the lights go out, or crying passionately after each departing hero, "My father, my father, the chariot of Israel and the horsemen thereof"? Nay, let the example of Elisha teach us. The question of the hour is on the character and the aspiration of the younger men. What may we hope for from them? What are their own hopes and what their aspirations?

As I ask this question, "What are the young men doing? Are they in training for these places? Will they fill them in their time?" I hear two answers coming back from opposite quarters, and neither one of these answers seems the truest or the wisest. On the one hand I hear the answer of depression, uttering that saddest of all words, "Degeneration;" saying, "The sons are falling below the stature of their fathers in physique, in intellectual fibre, in moral vigor. They are more afraid of hardship and more in love with ease; more narrow, more selfish, more self-indulgent, more frivolous, more materialistic. We cannot look for another Washington, nor for another Sherman, for not only they but the making of them has passed away. Henceforward we must look for a civilization more splendid than the world has ever seen, but inhabited by diminished men, by men growing to believe that there are things which justify a man in selling his soul, and that a man's life may consist in the abundance of the things that he possesseth."

On the other hand I hear the answer of over-confidence; the pride which issues from blended inexperience and materialism; and the answer of this over-confidence implies, if it does not say, that young men are destined surely to outstrip their fathers in attaining the grand prize of life. The answer of this over-confidence entrenches itself within the fortifications of one single and supreme argument, and from that entrenchment no controversy can dislodge it. That argument is the splendor and the completeness of modern civilization. One ventures to breathe a doubt as to whether the places of the great departed are being filled or only tenanted by their successors; whether examples of grand and consummate self-sacrifice and of the worship of duty are as frequent as of old, and the answer is given back, "Yes, but see our civilization; contrast it with the ways in which our fathers lived; see how swiftly we do things; see how magnificently we do things; see these great buildings; see our wealth."

Not with either of these answers am I in sympathy; not surely with the answer of depression, which sees only in the manhood of our younger men degeneration from the parental type; and not, as surely, with the answer of over-confidence, which often is far more depressing than the other by reason of its too evident exaltation over purely material abundance, and its unconscious inability even to conceive the type, the *esprit*, of true, unselfish, uncommercial greatness.

Between these two extremes of depression and of over-confidence lies the true position for the younger men to take as the fathers are leaving us and ascending to their reward; and I would to God my words might be blessed to-day, as a revealing of the truth and the worthiness of this position to even one whose views of life are yet open to influence, and as an encouragement to those who have already taken this position as their own. To believe only in degeneration would be pessimism; to believe only that we are greater than our fathers because in some points we live more comfortably, and in many points we work more rapidly, would be to indulge a most shallow fancy. From each of these positions we are drawn to a better and a wiser mind by the glorious associations of this day. As we younger men think to-day of the great departed, of those two with whom this day is especially connected (with one as his first day of earthly life, with the other as his first day of rest in the grave); as we think of all the others who have gone, leaving vast vacancies for us to fill, vast ministries for us to perpetuate; as we cry after them, " Our fathers, our fathers, the chariots of Israel and the horsemen thereof;" and as we ask ourselves, "Are we training for their places? Are we worthy of them?"—let the recognition of departed greatness draw us, with Elisha, to the true position. The recognition of greatness is next in rank to the possession of it. And the true position is one of wholesome courage mixed with wholesome fear. This is a great time in which to live. And every man of thought is bound, with wholesome courage, to recognize its greatness. There are conditions promoting success denied to our fathers. The more shame to us if, with a fair, fighting chance, we do not succeed. There are grand activities, present and accessible, which were not dormant, but uncreated and unimagined, when Washington finished his lifework, and when Sherman was born. There are grand liberties of speech and liberties of action; there are grand vocations which to men of spirit are callings in very deed, — callings Divine, which angels might envy but cannot share. Ah! if there is degeneration anywhere, it is not in the possibilities for the men, but in the men for the possibilities.

But it is also a time of grievous peril, — peril beyond language for the men who have not in youth caught their inspiration directly and sincerely from that Greatest of the Ascended Heroes, even from Him "Who is the Way and the Truth and the Life."[1] I hardly know how they can escape degeneration, for the peril of the age has three modes of expression, and through one or another of these modes it seems certain to capture and diminish the man whose eye is not set upon the far-beaming Face of Christ. The peril of the age is materialism. And its three modes of expression are the materialism of pleasure, the materialism of business, the materialism of unbelief.

The materialism of pleasure! He who is captured by it is degenerated toward the stature of a pigmy manhood, soft, effeminate, feebly self-indulgent; his thoughts revolve in orbits more and more circumscribed; he loses steadily the glorious force centrifugal which pours outward from himself towards others; he becomes centripetal; energy works inward, growing self-absorbent, — a diminishing man!

The materialism of business! He who is captured by it grows in inverse ratio to his success. Business must increase, but he must decrease; each year more selfish, more pitiless, more proportionately illiberal. Life means for

---

[1] St. Jno. xiv. 6.

him more and more its equivalent in dollars; and the symmetry of manhood perishes through the abnormal growth of the commercial instinct.

The materialism of unbelief! He who is captured by it falls into the consummate, secret snare of modern degeneration. Nothing robs life of potential heroism more certainly than the surrender of faith in the spiritual and the unseen. Nothing diminishes the size of character like the renunciation of faith's eternal and infinite aspirations. The materialism of unbelief not only puts out the lamps and the altar fire within the sanctuary, it builds up with dead masonry eastward and westward the windows through which we have looked out upon the Face of God. "My father, my father, the chariot of Israel and the horsemen thereof: of such as thee are the true heroes made,— who through faith subdued kingdoms, wrought righteousness, obtained promises, stopped the mouths of lions; out of weakness were made strong, waxed valiant in fight, turned to flight the armies of the aliens." Amen.

XIX.
THE GLORY OF YOUNG MEN.

XIX.

THE GLORY OF YOUNG MEN.

PREACHED AT WILLIAMS COLLEGE, MARCH 8, 1891.

"The glory of young men is their strength." — PROVERBS xx. 29.

EVERYTHING which God has made possesses, when in its normal state, a glory or a beauty of its own, and peculiar to itself. "There is one glory of the sun, and another glory of the moon, and another glory of the stars."[1] The glory of the sea is its depth, its immensity, and its power. The glory of the flower is its coloring and its fragrance. The glory of the opal is the mysterious water in its heart, gleaming like the reflection of fire. The glory of little children is their profound guilelessness and their sacred helplessness. The glory of the aged is their chastened sweetness, their subduing calmness, their "gray-haired might." "The glory of young men is their strength."

Strength is a relative term in respect of de-

[1] 1 Cor. xv. 41.

gree. The buffalo as he plunges over the prairie is strong; the lark as he rises for his matin hymn is strong; the forester as he swings the ponderous axe is strong; the barnacle as it clings to the ship's bottom is strong. Strength is a variable term in respect of applied meaning. The advocate makes a strong argument for his client. The physician administers a strong tonic to his patient. The composer creates a strong melody. The locksmith forges a strong bolt. The artist sketches a strong profile.

In dealing with a word so relative and so variable as the word "strength," what shall determine the sense in which it is used when presented to us as the peculiar ornament and beauty of young men? The nature of the thing to which the term is applied must fix the sense in which the term is used. We do not confuse the strength of the buffalo with the strength of the lark, because we carry distinct impressions concerning the natures of these two creatures. "The glory of young men is their strength." If we take young manhood as a work of God, and consider it in its normal state, of what nature do we find it to be, — a simple nature or a complex nature? The block of quartz has a simple nature; we may hammer it, crush it, weigh it, and we do not find it in the last analysis to possess any other nature than the nature of matter. The tropical orchid has a simple nature. We may dissect it, magnify it, or propagate it, but it never discloses to us any other nature than the nature of matter. But when we take a good normal specimen of young manhood and examine it, we find instantly in our specimen the signs of a complex nature.

We find, first of all, a physical nature: a nature of matter; a bodily personality, which, in the normal specimen, corresponds to one of the many meanings of strength, and which, in so far as it in any measure approximates completeness, is approximately strong. It is a splendid organism, fearfully and wonderfully made, capable of uses that touch almost every point in the entire arc of possibility, from the most sacred to the most profane. We find, in the second place, a nature of feeling and impulse and reason, a mental and emotional personality, which in the normal specimen corresponds to another of the many meanings of strength. In this nature (i. e. in the mental and emotional man) lie the will, the natural affections, the reasoning powers; and, as we can immediately see, — although this is not the body, although we can think of the mental man apart from the physical man, — these two natures are in fact intricately connected.

We find, in the third place, a nature of spirit: a spiritual nature, which, in the normal specimen, is capable of receiving impressions from God, and of communicating with Him through an answering life; a nature which God can work upon by His Spirit, finding in it capacities to which He can reveal truths that no being who had not this nature could possibly understand. In the physical nature there are elements which, to some extent, other animals hold in common with man. In the mental and emotional nature there are apparently elements of feeling and even of intention which, in some rudimentary sense that we may not be able to define, certain animals, like dogs and horses, seem to possess in common with man. But in his spiritual nature man has a nature all his own. This is his $\pi\nu\varepsilon\nu\mu\alpha$ — his spirit, — which answers to the Spirit of God, and which constitutes him, whether or not he has become in character at all like God, a creature who is made in the Image of God.

As a result of our investigations we find, therefore, that this normal specimen of young manhood which we are for the present examining has not a simple nature, like the block of quartz or like the tropical orchid. He has a complex nature, which is like himself, and like himself alone, in this, that it is a threefold nature, or a triad of natures, — three natures in one person. He is the body-man, with full bodily powers. He is the mind-man, with will and feeling and thought-life. He is the spirit-man, with the potential gift of understanding the communications of God, and of communicating with God in his turn. This being what he is, this being the nature of young manhood, if "the glory of young men is their strength" that strength must be of an order corresponding to the nature of that creature of whom it is the characteristic and the peculiar glory. The glory of young men in their normal state, as God means them to be, must therefore be a strength that corresponds in its expansiveness to the complex nature of which it becomes, in the order of God's choice, the most beauteous ornament. It must be a strength expressing itself, so far as possible, in the completeness of physical life, so far as possible in the completeness of mental and emotional life, so far as possible in the completeness of spiritual life. Now, if we have thus far reasoned correctly, we have brought the subject just where we want it to be, broadly into that foreground where we can look upon young manhood in the fulness of its great threefold life.

And here we may with safety leave the subject for a brief moment, whilst we turn to define strength; and then we will proceed to apply the defined word to the threefold manhood of young men as their peculiar glory.

Any lover of the meanings of words will understand the fascination of tracking a great word back to its birthplace. It awakens somewhat of the same feelings which we have had on visiting the birthplace of a great man. At least twenty-five different Hebrew words are, in the Old Testament, translated into the single English equivalent, "strength." As you may suppose, every possible shade of meaning is thus presented. The word which we find in our text, descriptive of that peculiar type of strength which is the glory of young men, is a singularly suggestive and a singularly magnificent word. In the three languages, the Arabic, the Syriac, and the Hebrew, we trace back the cognate forms of this word, and the parent stem of all we find to be a very ancient verb, meaning "to pant," as one pants for breath who is exerting every power in some great contest. Instantly a picture is brought before the mind, that, in the days in which we live, is intelligible to every young man; a picture as of one who has set himself a difficult task which will call for every ounce of strength and of pluck within reach; who has brought into play his very best energies; who is honestly and gloriously taxed, and whose breath comes quick with earnestness as he faces the issue before him, determined to dare and to do, even to the uttermost. That is the stem of this strong word, — the panting for breath which comes with all exacting and resolute effort; and then, as we trace the word down, we find that it always contemplates a victory of some sort to be won. It is not the strength of mere dogged endurance apart from any special end in view. It keeps the end in view, always an overcoming, always a victory in sight. It is the strength of him who pants to be a conqueror. And this, says the writer of the Proverbs, — this is the glory of young men. As the sun has its peculiar glory of light and warmth; as the sea has its peculiar glory of immensity and depth; as childhood has its glory of guilelessness; as age has its glory of reverend and chastened dignity, — so young manhood, in its normal state, has for its peculiar beauty and charm that strength which is the panting of the earnest and resolute life to win its victory.

If this, then, is the nature of that strength, a panting for victory, which is the glory of young men, it is our privilege to point out how this selfsame principle of strength will, in the absolutely normal life, reveal itself in each of the three natures which, in a manner so unique and so sublime, are incorporated in the personality of young manhood. And as we proceed we shall see how evidently this glorious strength-gift, this panting after victory which is the peculiar charm of a rightly constituted young manhood, is God's wise provision to fit young manhood to cope with the difficulties it must encounter; to live above the temptations by which it must be assailed; to win the prizes which shall enrich all the after-life. God has given, as youth's peculiar vantage, this panting after victory, because, in this world of adversities, such are the stumbling-blocks, physical, mental, spiritual, in the path of success, such are the odds against success, it is necessary to pant for victory before you can gain it.

This panting for victory reveals itself in the threefold constitution of young manhood. In the physical nature it reveals itself in the love of exercises and contests that test nerve and muscle, and in the reverent preservation of health. It is a great pity that any excesses or other perversions of athletic sports should have drawn down upon them unfavorable criticisms from any quarter, for in their essence, in their relation to the glory of young men, and in their connection with a complete philosophy of young manhood, athletic sports and exercises are truly noble and truly necessary. Effeminate and deficient would be the people that had no outdoor games, and the race of young men who took no interest, direct or indirect, in physical contests and exercises. If we spoke only of the effect of these contests in creating a sentiment which encourages the more careful preservation of health, we should be amply justifying their continuance: for when one thinks of the perils which must be met even by the young man who has no self-destroying habits; when we remember how many in their early years, and in exacting and unfavorable occupations, must fight hereditary taint, fever-germs, bad food, overwork, accidents, and God only knows what more beside, — it is good to have a sentiment in the air that even physical strength is the glory of young men.

But I see much more than this in that panting for victory which, in the young man of normal condition, leads him in some form or other, direct or indirect, to take interest in things that test nerve and try muscle, and that maintain health. This enthusiasm for physical contests and exercises is God's law working itself out in one branch of the young man's nature; and even if sickness or deformity have shut him out from these fine contests and these exhilarating exercises, he can show that he is true in spirit to that law by loving and applauding the victories of others.

In the mental and emotional nature this strength which is the panting for victory reveals itself in the intellectual and financial ambitions and in the pure affections of ardent youth. The glory of young men is the strength of their ambitions and the strength of their affections. It is normal to aspire. It is normal to love. The resolute worker and the resolute lover are alike fulfilling ends for which they were created. These mighty and holy efforts wrought through the ambitions and through the affections are, in so far as they accord with truth and with virtue, the operations of a law which sets at last upon the head of young manhood the crown of honor and dignity. This panting after victory in the realm of his life which contains the will, the affections, the reasoning powers; this earnestness which becomes at length written upon the very countenance, and which stands self-betrayed in the very tones of the voice, — has a meaning which reaches down into the foundations of character, and which clothes young manhood with a beautiful worthiness and power. It is the happy indication that he has taken the first step toward winning the victory, in his realizing so profoundly that there is a victory to be won.

In the spiritual nature, this strength which is the panting for victory reveals itself in the panting of the soul for communion with God. The symmetry of life is unknown till this transpires. Can we call it strength of a kind that is worthy to be known as the glory of young men, until this strength has shown itself in the highest realm of the man's nature, even in that realm in which he is touched by the Life of God, and in which he touches God in return? Can we speak of the man as strong, as panting after victory, when he is only an athlete, or only an ambitious man, and is not a man who is reaching outward and upward for fellowship with his Divine Father and his Divine Saviour?

No, I cannot call him strong. I may admire him as a fearless athlete, ever ready for the contest which tries nerve and muscle; or I may admire him as a man of ambition, or as a man of talent, or as a man of affection, showing in his work and in his love most praiseworthy earnestness; but I cannot call him strong when, on that side of his nature which is undoubtedly the loftiest, — on the side which he presents to God, — he appears to be destitute of ambition, and to know nought of what it means to pant for that victory which overcomes the world. I call him strong, with that strength which is the glory of young men, who, in addition to all physical and mental ambitions, is conscious that he pants for a nobler life as the servant of God; is conscious that he has in him an immortal principle which can express itself, and which can fulfil itself, only in communion with God; is conscious that nothing can satisfy his deepest life, or bring to him the highest conception of victory, but the growth of character into the likeness of God. I call this man strong with that strength which is the essential glory of young men, whether as yet he has found peace in Christ or not. I call him strong, for the strength is manifesting itself in his highest selfhood, in the panting for a spiritual victory. He may not yet have been able to get his hand consciously upon Christ. He may to-day be only groping after Christ, or he may be holding Christ very blindly and uncertainly. Nevertheless he is panting for victory, and he is awake to the knowledge of his own nature as one bearing God's Image; he recognizes the claim of God upon his life; he realizes that " none of us liveth to himself and no man dieth to himself." [1] And to-day, as a Christian, or as a man desiring to be a Christian, he is conscious of a great spiritual purpose which has arisen in his life, which is suggesting to him spiritual action, which is beginning to shine like a pillar of fire, and to lead him on toward spiritual victory.

Thus have we considered that strength which is the glory of young men. It is in essence the panting for victory; and, in the man who is truly strong, it expresses itself in every part of his life, giving unity and symmetry to his manhood. In his physical nature it shows in the enthusiasm for a strong physical life; in his intellectual and emotional nature it shows in the intensity of his worthy ambitions and affections; in his spiritual nature it shows in his aspiration to rise above all that is

[1] Rom. xiv. 7.

unworthy of a child of God, and to attain a true communion and fellowship of daily life with the Life of God. Thus, in the highest and fullest sense, the glory of young men is their strength; that love of victory, that enthusiasm for the thought of overcoming, that high-minded earnestness which fits them, in proportion as they live a normal life, to cope with the difficulties that are the peculiar trial and discipline of their time of age. I look with unalterable and unspeakable affection upon young men. I cannot but feel that my companionship with them has in some faint degree enabled me to realize their sorrows and their joys, their failures and their victories. And it is because a most tender feeling goes forth alike to those who seem in any part of their life to lack their due proportion of that strength, that earnestness which is the glory of young men, and to those who are with any measure of completeness showing it forth, I desire also to speak a few words concerning the Destroyers and the Makers of Earnestness.

What are the great Destroyers of Earnestness? Is not one of them Self-indulgence? Does a man realize the extent of the damage he is doing to his manhood when he yields himself up to a lax and self-indulgent life?

No! surely he does not realize it, or he would never do it. It cannot be that he knows how, all the way on through the coming years, he must take a lower place than he might have taken, and live a weaker life than he might have lived, because of this, and this, and this, in which he has sluggishly and idly permitted habits of self-indulgence to fasten themselves like barnacles upon him.

Is not another Destroyer of Earnestness the severing of principle from life-work? What will more completely kill earnestness, and rob young manhood of its peculiar, high-minded strength, than the inner consciousness of having left moral principle behind on entering one's life work; of having made one's business life a mere wage-earning and not a calling, in which, whatever it may be, one is striving in every sense of the word " to be true to the best one knows "? " No man can serve two masters: for either he will hate the one and love the other, or else he will hold to the one and despise the other." [1] Christ has said this to us, and who does not know in his own heart that it is true! To do business on any other basis than that of the highest principle one knows, is to strike a death-blow at the earnestness of character.

[1] St. Matt. vi. 24.

And is not another Destroyer of Earnestness the surrender of our ideals? How many a man has surrendered his ideals simply because others told him they were too high! And that which makes it such a temptation to men to surrender their ideals, and so to lose their strength, is that they have not yet seen the True Ideal clearly; they lack a clear view of Him Who is the Only True Ideal of character. Christ is not before their eyes as their Master, Saviour, Friend, and Example. If He were so before their eyes and in their thoughts, they would not find it so easy to surrender the ideal; for following Him in preference to following the base notions of unspiritual minds would be found such a joyous and comforting thing amidst the hardships and temptations of the world, they would not, at any price, surrender the One Whose power had made life worth living.

And what are some of the Makers of Earnestness, the Makers of Strength? One is the acceptance of hardship as part of the contract; another is the thought of all those who have overcome.

One is, I say, the acceptance of hardship as part of the contract. "Thou, therefore, endure hardness, as a good soldier of Jesus Christ." [1] A man shrinks from breaking off a physical habit because it means hardship; he shrinks from noble intellectual training, because it means hardship; he shrinks from coming bravely forth and acknowledging himself to be a true soldier of Christ, because it means hardship. Of course it means hardship; but what then? Let him accept hardship as part of the contract, and he has discovered one of the deepest secrets of moral earnestness. He has caught Christ's meaning when He said: "In the world ye shall have pressure; but be of good cheer, I have overcome the world." [2]

And let him think, oh, let him think! of all those who have overcome. Let him remember how many a young man in times past has gone up this noble path before him. He is not the first; no, nor will he be the last. He is only one brave, true heart; only one clean, strong life, of all who have been, of all who shall be, of the younger soldiers, serving Christ fearlessly in the glory of their strength. Amen.

[1] 2 Tim. ii. 3.
[2] St. Jno. xvi. 33 (Latin version).

XX.
THE INTERPRETER.

XX.

THE INTERPRETER.

PREACHED AT THE HILL SCHOOL, POTTSTOWN, PA., JUNE 21, 1891.

"An interpreter : one among a thousand."— JOB xxxiii. 23.

As I stand in your midst once more, dear younger brothers of the Hill School, my heart fills with hope, with joy, and with desire. I pray that it may not be in vain I speak to you this day about the highest of all callings. What is the highest of all callings? You see a thousand people fighting the battle of life; some are gaining, some are losing, some are rising, some are stumbling. You look in their faces, and they are the faces of the average. You look in their lives, and they are the lives of the average, filled up with the usual things. But at last you find one face and one life that differs from the rest. How? In that face there is more of the shining of the Light of God; in that face there is more of the mark of higher thought and larger purpose; in that life there is a power: what power? the power to make others think larger thoughts and live larger lives. Among nine hundred and ninety-nine faces, and nine hundred and ninety-nine lives, that one face, that one life, shines like a beautiful light. You forget others, you remember it. What will you call that face, — that life? Call it " an interpreter, one among a thousand." To be an interpreter, — to be the one, among a thousand, to whom it is given to think out some thought which others have not understood; to live out some truth which others have not grasped; to find out some power which others have not known; to hold out some light which others have not perceived, and so to make the meaning of life clearer and the way of life brighter for some of the nine hundred and ninety-nine, — this is the highest of all callings.

" An interpreter, one among a thousand." I wish to-day to say four things about the interpreter. First, he is one of God's instruments. Second, he is always needed in the world. Third, he must be trained. Fourth, he must be called.

The interpreter is one of God's instruments. God teaches the many through the few. He takes one among a thousand, whispers a truth in his ear, and sets him to tell it to the nine hundred and ninety-nine. The highest, grandest knowledge the world has to-day has come to it through interpreters; the thousand did not find it out for themselves. God whispered His great thought to the one, and the one explained it to the many. If you look into the history of the higher forms of human knowledge you will find that the knowledge which to-day is the property of all intelligent people came through the interpreters, the few among the thousands who, in one department and another, caught the meaning of some hitherto undiscovered truth and told that meaning forth to men.

Let me illustrate this from the fields of science and art. Darwin was an interpreter, one among a thousand; it was given to him to see the meaning of that struggle for existence, forever going on in the animal kingdom, through which the evolution of species proceeds through a long series of upward or downward steps. And the truth that was whispered in his ear, by Him Who is the Source of all wisdom, he interpreted to thousands upon thousands of eager minds. Edison is an interpreter, one among a thousand. It was given to him to see a new world of possibility in the applications to human enterprises of that mysterious element of electricity. What he saw, what was whispered in his ear, he has explained to his fellow-men. Beethoven was an interpreter, one among a thousand. He was a creative musician. God whispered in his ear, deaf as it was to earthly sound, new possibilities of musical expression, and his writings became, to countless human minds, interpretations of emotions and aspirations previously unexpressed. Wordsworth was an interpreter, one among a thousand. Until his time, few people had thought much about the beauties of nature as expressions of the glorious life and love of God. But God whispered in Wordsworth's ear that new and higher view of the meaning of nature, its trees and flowers, its lakes, its mountains, its "trailing clouds," and the thought that was given him he interpreted to his fellow-men; and the influence of his interpretation we all feel to some extent; for that admiration and love of nature which is so strong in us is to be traced back to the influences that were set at work in the English-speaking world when Wordsworth's poems unfolded the long-unappreciated beauties of the earth.

But when we turn from these great interpreters of science and art to those still greater who have interpreted to mankind the very Nature of God, we find how true it is that God chooses to teach the many through the few. The apostle Paul was an interpreter, one among a thousand; an interpreter of the Person and work of Christ. God whispered in his soul the real essence of the truth of the gospel, which is Jesus Christ and Him crucified, — the mystery which had been hid from ages and generations, the power of Christ's Blood to take away sin; and Paul interpreted the gospel in that series of letters which for almost nineteen hundred years have been the guidebook of men upon this subject. The apostle John was an interpreter, one among a thousand, an interpreter of the love of God. Christ gave him such a glorious training by choosing him to be His Own dearest friend, by loving him as only one great soul can love another; and the message was whispered in the very depths of the soul of John, "God is love," and he through his epistle and gospel is interpreting that truth to-day to thousands upon thousands of souls, for whom it is putting a new meaning into life, and a new motive also. But I must go one step higher yet; I must remind you that Christ is an Interpreter, the Interpreter to our understandings of the Nature and Character of the invisible God. John wrote of Him these wondrous words: "No man hath seen God at any time: the Only Begotten Son, which is in the bosom of the Father, He hath declared Him." The Greek word for "declared" might well be translated "interpreted." Christ by taking upon Him our nature, and by manifesting Himself before men, interpreted to us the Nature and Character of the unseen Father, so that He says, "He that hath seen Me hath seen the Father."

Now, my younger brothers, I have carried you up to the highest illustration of the truth that the interpreter is one of God's instruments, and that so God has ever taught the many through the few. I will only say further on this point that it is true to-day as ever it was. To-day we see the interpreter, the one among a thousand. We see him wherever any human soul, having more of God's light upon it and more of life's meaning revealed to it than those around it have, is thinking out some thought which others have not understood, is living out some truth which others have not grasped, is finding out some power which others have not known, is holding out some light which others have not perceived, and so is making the meaning of life clearer and the way of life brighter for some of the nine hundred and ninety-nine.

The interpreter is always needed in the world. Not infrequently it happens in the world of labor that men are thrown out of employment through changes in the way of doing things: when the steam-power loom was invented, it threw the workers of the hand-loom out of business; when the railway mail service was invented, it threw the old mounted mail-carriers out of business. But the interpreter is always needed in the world. He into whose ear God has whispered the deeper, grander meaning of life; he who is able to show in his own person a wiser, loftier, usefuller way of living, — is always needed; there is always a place for him, there is always a work for him, for he is an interpreter, one among a thousand. Yes, younger brother, if God shall whisper in your ear that which shall make you in any sense an interpreter, if He shall fill you with any thought that others have not understood, you will realize, when an experience of the world has become yours, when a knowledge of its sin, its selfishness, its unbelief has dawned upon you, you will realize that amidst the myriads of men and women and children that crowd the cities and spread over the country, that surge by you in the streets, that throng you in the railway trains, that buy and sell, and laugh and weep, that stand and fall, that sing and suffer, nine hundred and ninety-nine out of the thousand do not seem to know what the true meaning of life is. Their eyes are set on other things than the glory of the service of God. Their ears are filled with other sounds than the whispers of the Voice of God. Their hands are oftener closed with grasping than opened for helping. And what they need is an interpreter, one among a thousand, who has seen with the eyes of faith a grander way of living, who has heard with the ears of love the sound of greater music; they need an interpreter to tell them the meaning of life. But this is not all. You will find not only how few know the meaning of life, you will find how few know how to live. The nine hundred and ninety-nine do not know how to take care of their bodies, how to take care of their minds, how to take care of their spirits. The reason they do not realize the meaning of life, and the glory of the service of God, is because they have let themselves in some way go to waste. They have wasted themselves physically, by breaking laws of nature and permitting unchecked indulgences; or they have wasted themselves mentally, by refusing the discipline of the mind and surrendering their intellects to weak and trivial influences; or they have wasted themselves spiritually, by resisting the Spirit of God and loving darkness rather than light. And what they need is an interpreter, — some one in whose ear God has whispered the sanctity of the body, and the holy care of it; the dignity of the mind and the broader culture of it; the glory of the human spirit, and its fellowship with the Spirit of God. Yes, the interpreter will never be thrown out of business. The ways of doing things may change; the laws of trade may change; the canons of literature may change; the *modus operandi* of science may change, — but a place for him always remains, a need for him always exists: as long as the generations of men are born, he is needed in whose ear God has whispered the true meaning of life and the true way of life, that he may interpret these to the nine hundred and ninety-nine.

The interpreter must be trained. He is a specialist; he is one among a thousand. His calling is to show to some fellow-being, perhaps to many, new light in the science of living. This he cannot do unless, like every specialist, he knows more in his department than the average know. Like every specialist, then, he must be trained. The question then, is, What is the training of an interpreter? In answering this question let us bear in mind what this interpreter is to do; bearing this in mind, it is easy to say what his training is to be. Now what is he to do? He is to be one whose life, in its spirit and in its method, is to be the means of showing other people what the meaning of life is, and what the best way to live is. Consequently the training of this interpreter must be, I should say, these three things: to know himself, to know the meaning of life, and to walk with God.

To know himself, — this is part of the training of an interpreter. He who does not understand himself is not likely to be one through whose influence others learn to understand themselves. The interpreter of life is a close student of his own life; he studies the forces that are at work in himself; he studies himself as if he were some one else; he acknowledges that his own being is a great mystery of contrary forces; but he says, with God's help, " I propose to understand this mystery, to see the relation of these contrary forces which are in me, to find the clue which will bring order out of this confusion, and peace out of this great unrest."

To know the meaning of life, — this is part of the training of an interpreter. What is the meaning of life? The meaning of life is the service of God, in thought, in word, and in deed. How can the interpreter interpret the meaning of life to others unless he is perfectly sure of what the meaning of life is? This, then, is part of his training : to realize the service of God in all thoughts, in all words, in all deeds ; to be constantly under the influence of the idea that life means the service of God ; to accustom himself to the idea until he takes it into account continually in making all his decisions, in conducting all his operations, in using and caring for his body, his mind, and his spirit, from day to day.

To walk with God, — this is part of the training of an interpreter. He is to make God real to others as the object of service in thought, in word, and in deed. How can he make God real to others unless God is real to himself? And how can God be real to himself unless he walks with God in his own daily life; unless he keeps up a constant, earnest, truthful fellowship with God? Unless he walks with God in his own secret life, he cannot be an interpreter of God and of life. He will become only one of the nine hundred and ninety-nine who do not walk with God, and who are not interpreters; and some one else God will choose for an interpreter, whispering in his ear.

Yes, the interpreter must be trained; while he is still young, while he has still time, and before the evil days come when manhood's heart is hardened, he must be trained to know himself, to know the meaning of life, to walk with God.

The interpreter must be called. Perhaps you think I have got things in the wrong order; that I should have put the calling before the training. I think not. If we had to be sure of our calling before we went into training, not many would go into training. But we are sure that we cannot be interpreters unless we are trained to know ourselves, to know the meaning of life, to walk with God. Therefore we give ourselves to this glorious training, and we leave the calling with God, trusting Him to call us whither He will, and to make us interpreters of life whensoever He will, and to whomsoever He will. And I think the greatest thing about this calling to be an interpreter is, one may have it unconsciously. I know that some of those who have interpreted to me the meaning of life, and the nobler ways of living, were unconscious of their call. They knew not that they were God's interpreters. They only thought of their training. With lowly, loving, and obedient hearts they were seeking to know themselves, to know the meaning of life and truthfully to walk with God; but the calling was on them, though they knew it not, and by living they revealed to others the way to live.

I look before me upon this group of boyish faces; I follow you forth into the years that widen before you. I ask myself with deepest curiosity, Who among them will be interpreters? As I ask, there rise before my mental vision three pictures from the olden time, which tell me what forms of interpretation may be in store for some of you, — the calling of one and another. I see the palace of Pharaoh in the kingdom of Egypt. I see fear and distress written on the countenance of the king. A dream has burned itself upon his imagination, the import of which he cannot grasp, and none of the magicians in his court can tell him what it means. I see the free-hearted, white-souled Joseph summoned before the throne, and the royal dreamer pleading with him: "I have dreamed a dream, and there is none that can interpret it, and I have heard say of thee that thou canst understand a dream to interpret it."

I hear the modest answer of the young interpreter: "It is not in me; God shall give Pharaoh an answer of peace."[1] Younger brothers, shall it be the calling of some of you to go forth, and like Joseph, by God's help, interpret to men their own thoughts? Souls to-day are dreaming dreams whose import they do not understand; thinking confusedly, catching glimpses of truth amidst forests of error. Shall one of you help others to read the meaning of their thoughts, to understand the message of God's Spirit in their own hearts?

I see another picture. It also is the picture of a palace, — a hall filled with revelry, — the banquet of the dissolute Belshazzar. He sits, a spectacle of despair, his knees smiting together with fear, his eyes riveted on the handwriting that has suddenly appeared upon the wall. To tell him its meaning his own astrologers are powerless. He turns to the fearless youth of Daniel and cries: "I have heard of thee, that thou canst make interpretations and dissolve doubts; now, if thou canst read the writings, and make known to me the interpretation thereof, thou shalt be clothed with scarlet and have a chain of gold about thy neck, and shalt be the third ruler in the kingdom."[2] And Daniel,

[1] Gen. xli. 1–43.   [2] Dan. v. 1–30.

girded with the courage of God, has strength to tell that man of sin the meaning of the handwriting on the wall; that he has destroyed himself, that he has been weighed in the balance and found wanting, that he must reap what he has sown. Younger brothers, shall it be the calling of some of you to go forth, and like Daniel, speak plainly to men about their sinful lives, interpret to men who are living in sin the warnings of God, tell them that the life of indulgence shall be weighed and found wanting, snatch men from their self-destroying ways, as brands from the burning?

I see one other picture; not a palace, but a country roadside; not the glare of midnight lamps, but the sweet radiance of a Lord's Day afternoon: three men are there; two with burning hearts are listening; One, with the light of the Resurrection in His Divine Face, is preaching and interpreting the Holy Scriptures; and underneath my picture of the Emmaus road it is written, "And beginning at Moses and all the prophets, He expounded unto them in all the Scriptures the things concerning Himself."[1] Younger brothers, shall it be the calling of some of you, even like Him Who rose from the dead, to go

[1] St. Lk. xxiv. 13-32.

forth and walk by the side of your fellow-men, and open their understandings that they may understand the Scriptures, that they may grasp the things that concern Christ?

To the Christian boys in this school I would say this closing word. In this world, which knows so little of Jesus Christ, each Christian is called to be an interpreter of Christ, — one among a thousand. In the Gospel of Matthew it is written of our Lord, "They shall call His Name Emmanuel, which being interpreted is, God with us."[1] The Name of Emmanuel is borne by those of you who have confessed Christ. That Name, being interpreted, means "God with us." It is for each of you to interpret that Name to men; to show, by the truth, by the pureness, by the strength of your lives, that to be a Christian means, being interpreted, "God with us." Amen.

[1] St. Matt. i. 23.

www.ingramcontent.com/pod-product-compliance
Lightning Source LLC
Chambersburg PA
CBHW031425230426
43668CB00007B/445